THE PERICEO TOOL

TEAMS AND ORGANIZATIONS, DEVELOP YOUR CAPACITY FOR COLLECTIVE INTELLIGENCE

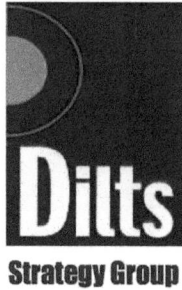

Strategy Group

Dilts Strategy Group

P. O. Box 67448

Scotts Valley CA 95067

USA

Phone: (831) 438-8314

E-Mail: info@diltstrategygroup.com

Homepage: http://www.diltstrategygroup.com

Library of Congress Control Number: 2019903473

I.S.B.N. 978-1-947629-41-7

THE PERICEO TOOL

TEAMS AND ORGANIZATIONS, DEVELOP YOUR CAPACITY FOR COLLECTIVE INTELLIGENCE

Robert Dilts

Elisabeth Falcone

Isabelle Meiss

Gilles Roy

Design and illustrations by Antonio Meza

Contents

Acknowledgments   1

Preface   3

Introduction   7

1- The Basic Principles of Collective Intelligence   9

1.1 Resonance - Synergy - Emergence   10

1.2 Intention   11

1.3 C.O.A.C.H.state and C.R.A.S.H. state   12

1.4 Holons and holarchies   13

1.5 Ego and soul   14

1.6 Aligning the logical levels (The Dilts Pyramid)   14

1.7 Vision - Mission - Ambition - Role   16

1.8 Modelling   16

1.9 Scorecards as a Modeling Tool   18

1.10 Framing   19

1.11 Dynamic Teaming and Revolving leadership   19

1.12 Meetings with Delegated Functions (Réunions Déléguées)   22

2 - Our approach: Synergy of three perspectives
(Disney's Imagineering strategy)   23

2.1 The Dreamer   27

   The aims of the study, our ambition   28

2.2 The Realist   29

   a. The organization   31

   b. The working community   32

Contents

c. The selection process   33

d. Putting the study into practice:
   Climbing the Collaboration Spiral.   35

e. The emergence of the tool   37

2.3. The Critic   41

a. Feedback and constructive criticism from business partners   41

b. Feedback and constructive criticism in collective workshop   44

2.4. What we learned from out own collective work   46

3 - The Tool: Process and representation
    Key Factors   48

3.1. Key Factors for Vision (Purpose)   50

3.2. Key Factors for Identity   51

3.3. Key Factors for Values and Beliefs   52

3.4. Key Factors for Capabilities   53

3.5. Key Factors for Behaviors   54

3.6. Key Factors for Environment   55

Conclusion   56

And now?   57

Afterword   58

Contents

Appendices

A0. Presentation of the Dilts Strategy Group (DSG) and the "Success Factor Modeling" (SFM™)   61

A1. Presentation of co-authors and illustrator   66

A2. Presentation of Formation Evolution and Synergy   75

A3. Presentation of VISION 2021   77

A4. Charter and ethical code for the PERICEO project   80

A5. Ethical Code of the Collective Intelligence Intervention for the consultants involved in the project   84

A6. Questions for PERICEO interviews   86

A7. The PERICEO training program   89

Bibliography   92

Acknowledgments

We warmly thank all the consultants who have participated at one time or another in this adventure, particularly those who have conducted the interviews with us:

Eric BAUDET, Florence BETITO, Carine CAMPOS

Jean-Luc CERVIA, Francis CLAVERIE, Yaël GRONNER

Nadia ANGLESY, Christine MARSAN, Jean-Pierre MELANI

Catherine PENA, Didier PERALDO, Nathalie ROCHAIX

Gilles VIALARD

This list is not exhaustive: different individuals got involved at different points in the modeling process, others joined us periodically during the various phases. We send all who were involved our sincere appreciation.

We especially want to thank Antonio Meza, to whom we owe the cover of this book and most of the illustrations in it: thank you for your availability, your kindness, the quality of your listening and the resulting representations! Also, Anne-Brigitte Lubrez, who proof read the French version of this book: thank you for your generosity, acuteness and the quality of your contribution, which have been invaluable to us. Finally, we give heartfelt thanks to Deborah Bacon Dilts: your discreet and caring presence throughout this adventure has brought us a lot of courage and sweetness. Thank you for your presence each time we needed it. Infinite gratitude!

Last but not least, our special thoughts go to the leaders and teams of the twenty-two companies who agreed to take part in the research project and thus allowed the model to emerge. Thank you for your trust, your contribution and the time you have given us.

Preface

Originally published in French (in 2018), this book is a manifestation of a dream that began about twenty years ago, at the end of the 1990s, when Robert Dilts and his brother, John Dilts, founded the "Dilts Strategy Group" and established the principles and processes of the Success Factor Modeling (SFM™). They were looking for answers to questions such as "what is the difference that makes the difference between successful projects, teams, entrepreneurs and ventures compared with those who are average or failing?" and "what are the key factors necessary to start and grow a successful and prosperous business?" (See Appendix A0).

At that time, Robert had already been working with companies and organizations for almost twenty years. Applying his experience with Neuro-Linguistic Programming, a methodology that identifies and applies the patterns of thought and behavior of exceptional performers, Robert had already written numerous books on leadership, innovation, effective communication, etc.

In their study of exceptional teams and companies, one of the major success factors Robert and John identified was what they called "generative collaboration." They noticed that, in companies that are particularly successful, people are able to work creatively and collectively to achieve their dreams and visions.

Many of the fundamental principles and processes of generative collaboration are described in the book *Success Factor Modeling Volume II, Generative Collaboration: Releasing the creative Power of Collective Intelligence* (2017). The models and practices presented in this work formed the basis for the innovative PERICEO project and the book you are now holding in your hands. This book was formulated and co-written, applying the processes of Collective Intelligence (CI), by four people – Elisabeth Falcone, Isabelle Meiss, Robert Dilts and Gilles Roy – through numerous exchanges between 2016 and 2017. All four of us share a passion for Collective Intelligence and a commitment to explore and experiment with new socio-professional paradigms. A detailed presentation of each of us can be found in the appendices at the end of the book (see Appendix A1).

In 2009, Gilles invited Robert and his wife Deborah (a longtime friend of Gilles) to Avignon to present a first seminar on Collective Intelligence. Between 2009 and 2011, Gilles, Robert and Deborah met several times and decided to choose Collective Intelligence as a platform from which to positively influence the world over the next ten years.

They entitled the project VISION 2021. Their plan involved conducting research and developing Collective Intelligence tools for businesses and social organizations, both local and international.

Applying René Dubos' principle to "think globally, act locally," Gilles, Robert and Deborah believed that changes would occur through education and action rather than through traditional politics. They organized a first three-year Collective Intelligence training course through Formation Evolution et Synergie, the training institute co-managed by Gilles and based in Avignon (see the presentation in the Appendix A2). The program brought together a group of 75 participants, including Isabelle and Elisabeth, and consequently formed an initial "skills and heart" network that brought the VISION 2021 project to life.

This association has grown to over 100 members and is deploying the principles and practices of Collective Intelligence in many directions. Each year, it organizes a Congress on Collective Intelligence and a Summer University. A detailed presentation is contained in the appendices at the end of this book (see appendix A3).

During this period, Robert was continuing to develop the applications of Success Factor Modeling, resulting in three independent and yet complementary training courses.

1) **Next Generation Entrepreneurs: "Live Your Dreams and Create a Better World Through Your Business"** is a program designed to help people to develop the skills and commitment necessary to launch a project based on their passion and vision by creating a "Circle of Success" for themselves, their customers, their collaborators, their stakeholders and their partners.

2) **Conscious Leadership and Resilience: "Orchestrating Innovation and Fitness for the Future"** refers to the capacities to inspire others and give meaning to their actions, to meet the challenges and rebound in the face of adversity. The program underlines the importance of creativity and endurance as major success factors in creating successful businesses that contribute positively to the world.

3) **Generative Collaboration: "Facilitating Collective Intelligence"** focuses on how to effectively support Collective Intelligence within groups and teams, creating conditions that allow people to work creatively and productively to fulfill their dreams and visions. The program is divided into 3 modules : 1) Creating generative collaboration - 2) Modeling synergies - 3) Activating the wisdom of crowds. This program served as the basis for the PERICEO project and this book. And since the beginning of the adventure, seven trainers have been certified and authorized by Robert to teach this Collective Intelligence Facilitator course around the world.

P.E.R.I.C.E.O or "Projet d'Etude et de Recherche en Intelligence Collective dans les Entreprises et les Organisations" (Project for Study and Research on Collective Intelligence in Companies and Organizations) began as one of the VISION 2021 work groups. This study was launched in the fall of 2013 as an application of the process of Success Factor Modeling in order to research the phenomenon of synergy in groups and teams. Its aim has been to make a field-based evaluation of the latest trends and ideas applied by the teams and organizations to promote synergies and develop Collective Intelligence, in order to address the challenges and take advantage of opportunities in the current economic environment.

A number of teams and companies were selected on the basis of their reputation, innovative operation and industry leadership to participate in modeling interviews. A structured process and interview methodology was developed to enable facilitators from Robert's Collective Intelligence training to carry out their work with consistency. A specific charter and code of ethics was established. They appear at the end of the book in the appendices (see A4 and A5). You will find the list of facilitators who conducted the interviews at the beginning of this book, in the Acknowledgments.

Some examples of questions asked during the interviews include (see appendix A6 for a detailed questionnaire):

* *What are the current challenges and opportunities the company or team is facing?*

* *How do they view and value Collective Intelligence as a key means to succeed in today's business environment?*

* *How do they modify their business strategy and management practices to encourage and increase Collective Intelligence?*

* *What specific steps have they implemented to support Collective Intelligence on a practical level?*

Much of the work consisted in analyzing all the interviews to find key patterns of success factors and to draft a preliminary model. This draft was then tested in different contexts and optimized. The consultants then returned to their representatives from the selected companies and gave them feedback, comparing their responses with the overall model. The consultants pointed out both the strengths and areas for development for the company with respect to fostering Collective Intelligence. These exchanges led to tailor-made interventions for the companies, making it possible to further enrich the P.E.R.I.C.E.O. study and develop methodologies to facilitate Collective Intelligence. It is the story of this adventure that forms the basis of this book. Our goal is to share our discoveries and encourage further research and experimentation.

Working together in groups and teams is becoming more and more common and is a key part of contemporary life and modern businesses. Developing skill in fostering Collective Intelligence is therefore an essential success factor for entrepreneurs and leaders, from early stage start-ups to large organizations with a long history.

For almost twenty years now, the principles, skills and models developed with the SFM™ (Success Factor Modeling) approach have been applied to boost growth and prosperity. When Robert and John began developing SFM™, their intention was not simply to provide knowledge about efficient business practices, but rather create a movement that would enrich people's lives and make the world a better place. This book is part of this broader vision that can be expressed as "creating a world to which people want to belong."

Introduction

Why are we talking about Collective Intelligence (CI) today?

Like many important and "evocative" terms, there have been almost as many definitions of Collective Intelligence as authors on the subject ... For instance Hiltz and Turoff (1978) define it as "a capacity to collectively make decisions which are at least as good or, if possible, better than any single member of the group could have achieved alone." For Smith (1994) CI means "that a group of human beings can carry out a task as if the group, itself, were a coherent, intelligent organism working with one mind, rather than a collection of independent agents." And Levy (1994) defines CI as "a universally distributed form of intelligence, constantly dynamic, coordinated in real time, and which produces a powerful mobilization of skills" (Malone and Bernstein, 2015, page 2).

Generally speaking, *intelligence* can be defined as "the ability to interact successfully with one's the world, especially in the face of challenge or change." Collective Intelligence, then, can be viewed as "*the shared intelligence of a group, which emerges from collaboration and communication between several individuals,*" manifested, for example, in the synergy and resilience of ecosystems or other phenomena such as high performing teams or "The Wisdom of the Crowds" (Surowiecki 2008).

In today's rapidly changing world, the capacity for collective intelligence is becoming increasingly vital. Fluctuations in economic conditions frequently force teams and organizations to change their way of operating in order to do more with less resources. At the same time, the acceleration of global trade, the digital revolution, a growing sense of loss of meaning and the need to move forward with confidence in a more and more uncertain environment, reinforce the need to develop new modes of collaboration. In this context, working together with others, in groups and teams, is an increasingly common and important part of contemporary business life – and doing it effectively is essential. In a recent interview on Forbes.com, journalist Dan Schawbel asked Adam Grant, professor at Wharton university[1], to explain why

---

1 Adam Grant is an associate professor at Wharton University, Pennsylvania. He is graduated from the University of Michigan and Harvard in psychology of organizations. Its research is about motivation, organization of work, behaviors of co-operation and mutual assistance. He has been honored as one of the best professors of Business School under 40 years of age and received the "Excellence in Teaching Award" for the quality of his teaching in Wharton. He is recognized as one of the most influential HR experts in the world and is the author of the best-seller *Give and Take*.

interacting with others is the new means to succeed, in which it is even more important today than in the past (https://www.forbes.com/sites/danschawbel/2016/02/02/adam-grant-why-you-shouldnt-hire-for-cultural-fit/#7fa8b3d37eba). Grant made the following response:

> *The world of work has become much more interdependent, making relationships and reputations increasingly important in shaping the innovative ideas, business opportunities, client referrals, and promotions that come our way. There are at least three major trends behind the rise in interdependence.*
>
> *First is the growth of project-based work: organizations are bringing people together to collaborate on temporary teams, making interaction skills particularly important in shaping the results these short-term groups achieve.*
>
> *Second is the shift from a manufacturing economy to a service and knowledge economy: four out of every five Americans work in service roles, where meeting the needs of clients and customers is a defining feature of success.*
>
> *Third is the advent of online social networks: we can now track the reputations of job applicants, potential business partners, and service providers by identifying common connections on LinkedIn and tracking their behavior on social media.*

Grant's answer reveals a lot about how the world has changed in recent years and why collaboration is an essential success factor. Each of the trends he defines clearly point to the importance of perceiving ourselves and interacting with others from the perspective of being part of a collective as opposed to merely a separate individual. Clearly, the capacity to work collaboratively together with others as a collective is crucial for organizational success.

As far as we are concerned and throughout our work, we will proceed from the following definition:

> *In human systems, Collective Intelligence relates to the ability of people in a team, group or organization, to think and act in an aligned and coordinated mode. Similar to the way that hydrogen and oxygen combine to form the third entity of 'Water', collective intelligence transforms separate individuals into a cohesive group and creates a team in which the whole is truly greater than the sum of its parts.*
>
> Robert Dilts 2016

Chapter 1

Basic principles of Collective Intelligence

As previously mentioned, there are almost as many definitions of collective intelligence as authors on the subject ... and we know from experience that, for effective communication, it is fundamental to clarify what we intend when we use a particular word, and what it means for the people involved: *Do we agree on what this word, this idea covers? Are we talking about the same thing?*

It therefore seems to us a priority here—without going into the detailed content that we provide in our courses or interventions on Collective Intelligence—to present as clearly as possible the fundamentals we believe in and that underpin our research. You will find references to these fundamentals later in the text, identifiable by an asterisk (*).

1.1 Resonance – Synergy – Emergence

Resonance refers to what brings us together; where we feel alike and connected; where we meet. If we don't take the time to detect where we have resonance with others, it is difficult to act collectively.

Resonance is the result of a type of mutual influence between systems or objects that are specially attuned to one another.

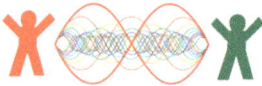

In groups, resonance refers to the degree to which members feel sense of alignment or connection with other group members' ideas, values and qualities. It involves discovering:

*   What is similar between us?
*   Where do we connect?

Synergy refers to our complementarities: the differences between us upon which we can capitalize. Synergy requires a certain degree of initial resonance. It becomes possible to create synergies when we are able to perceive our differences as an enrichment to common goals.

Synergy occurs when two (or more) things function together to produce a result that is not independently obtainable.

It requires an exchange of both information and energy in order to produce a result that includes and extends the individual contributions. Synergy results from exploring:

*   Where are our differences?
*   How can those differences complement one another?

Emergence results when the resonance and synergy between parts generates something new and unpredictable.

Emergence occurs when complex "patterns" appear as a result of relatively simple group interactions.

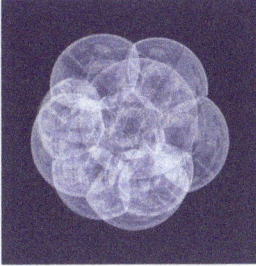

Emergent qualities are those that do not come directly from the components of a system but rather from how these components interact, i.e. when the whole is greater than the sum of its parts. Emergence arises from considering:

* What new could appear through our interactions?
* What else becomes possible?

A good analogy is that of a water molecule, which results from the integration of two atoms that originally had nothing to do with this molecule: hydrogen and oxygen.

1.2 Intention

> "*To the person who does not know where to go there is no favorable wind.*" ~ Seneca

In NLP, it is said that **our intention focuses our attention**. Our intention enables us to direct our energy towards an objective. Without a precise intention, we will not achieve anything specific and our energy will scatter in all directions.

To lead a constructive and fulfilled life requires us to evolve in a conscious way, by setting successive intentions and by focusing on their achievement.

It may be eye opening at this stage to draw a parallel with our smartphones and tablets. If we use them "off-line" they are disconnected from Bluetooth, wireless networks and from one another. They are unable to send, receive or "download" any new information. The same applies to us: to create the conditions for Collective Intelligence and generative collaboration, we must have our own psychological and physical "circuitry" in the proper state to go "on-line" with each other..

We call this state the COACH State.

1.3 COACH state and CRASH state.

COACH = Generative State - Channel Open – Online

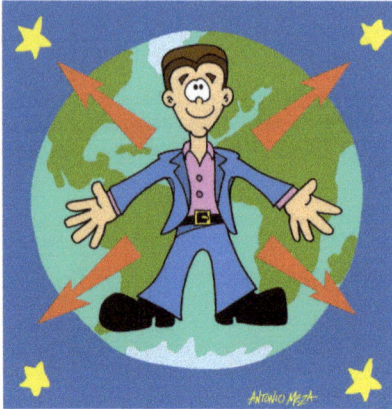

* **Center yourself**, especially in your belly center.

* **Open** your field of awareness.

* **Attend**, to what is going on within you and around you with awareness and mindfulness.

* **Connect** to yourself and to the larger systems you are part of.

* **Holding** everything that can happen from a state of resourcefulness and curiosity.

The opposite of this state we call CRASH state.

CRASH = Degenerative State - Channel Closed – Off line

* **Contracted**

* **Reactive**

* **Analysis Paralysis**

* **Separated**

* **Hostile/Hurting/Hating**

In a CRASH state, everything is "off line" and it is not possible to develop the connections necessary to produce Collective Intelligence.

1.4 Holons and Holarchies

A fundamental premise of generative collaboration and Collective Intelligence is expressed in the notions of "holons "and "holarchies" proposed by Arthur Koestler in the 1960s[2]

* **Holons**: each person is simultaneously a unique and separate whole, composed of other wholes, and part of larger wholes. Holons also have a "holographic" quality, such that the larger whole is in each part, and each part can recreate the whole.

* **Holarchy**: the dynamics of the relationships/interactions between holons. A holoarchy is an integrated hierarchy of semi-autonomous sub-wholes, consisting of sub-wholes, and so on. Each new larger whole both includes and transcends the parts on the level below it. It is important to emphasize that, in a holarchy, the lower levels are components necessary for all higher levels. If a lower level of the system is not present, the higher levels will not be able to be fully expressed. (As an example, without letters you are unable to make words.)

Each person is whole and part of a greater whole

2 Words and theory created by the novelist Arthur Koestler in his books (*The act of creation* and *Ghost in the machine*, 1964 and 1967). Reintroduced in 1997 by the writer and teacher of interpersonal psychology Ken Wilber in his book *A Brief History of Everything*. Also used in physics in the relativistic formulation of quantum theory of the fields. See Success Factor Modeling Volume I (pp.22-23) and Volume II (p. 8)

1.5 Ego and Soul

Taking into account the fact that each of us is a holon, our lives and motivations are driven by two complementary aspects of our identities: those emerging from our existence as (1) an independent and separate individual, and as (2) part of a larger whole (e.g.: family, profession, community, etc .).

We call "ego" the part of our existence that we experience as a separate whole. The part of our existence that we experience as a holon (part of a larger whole) can be referred to as our "soul." From our perspective, both of these aspects, ego and soul, are necessary for a healthy and successful existence.

The primary questions relating to our ego are about what we want to achieve for ourselves in terms our ambition and role. The primary questions with respect to the soul are those related to our vision and mission with respect to the larger systems of which we are a part.

1.6. Aligning the Logical Levels (The Dilts Pyramid)

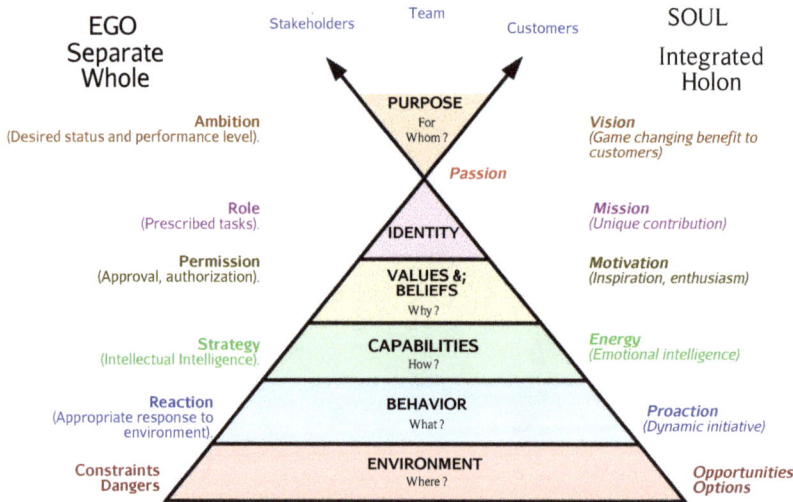

EGO
Separate
Whole

Stakeholders   Team   Customers

SOUL
Integrated
Holon

PURPOSE
For
Whom?

Ambition
(Desired status and performance level).

Vision
(Game changing benefit to customers)

Passion

IDENTITY

Role
(Prescribed tasks).

Mission
(Unique contribution)

VALUES &; BELIEFS
Why?

Permission
(Approval, authorization).

Motivation
(Inspiration, enthusiasm)

CAPABILITIES
How?

Strategy
(Intellectual Intelligence).

Energy
(Emotional intelligence)

BEHAVIOR
What?

Reaction
(Appropriate response to environment).

Proaction
(Dynamic initiative)

ENVIRONMENT
Where?

Constraints Dangers

Opportunities Options

"The concept of logical levels relates to the fact that certain processes and phenomena are created by the relationships between other processes and phenomena."

Any system of activities also constitute a subset within another system, which itself is embedded in another system, and so on. This type of relationship between systems produces processes that are located at different levels of the system in which we are operating. Our language, the structure of our brain, and our social systems illustrate these different levels and form hierarchies or levels of natural processes.

A simple example of this is the rate of change or the "speed" of a car. The speed depends on the distance covered by a vehicle in a given time (for example, 10 m / h). Thus, speed reflects the relationship between distance and time. The "velocity" of a car moving from the garage to the road is a different "level" from that of the car, the garage, the road or the clock, because it is a property of the relationship between them and does not exist without them.

Similarly, the "profitability" of a company is at a different level than that of the equipment used by this same company; and an idea is at a different level than that of the neurons of the brain producing it.

The concept of the logical levels of learning and change was first presented as a mechanism in behavioral sciences by anthropologist Gregory Bateson, who build on the research of Bertrand Russell in logic and mathematics.

According to Robert Dilts:

> The expression "logical levels", which I use in NLP, is inspired by the work of Bateson and refers to levels of processes hierarchically organized within an individual or group. The function of each level is to synthesize, organize and direct the interactions of the level immediately below it. Changing something at one of the higher levels would necessarily be expressed downward, precipitating changes on lower levels. Changing something at a lower level could eventually influence higher levels, but does not necessarily do so. These logical levels are composed (in top down order) of the following levels: (1) identity, (2), beliefs and values, (3) capabilities, (4) behaviors, and (5) environment. A sixth level, which can be called 'spiritual, can be defined as a type of 'relational field' embracing multiple identities that gives rise to a sense of belonging to a larger system, beyond the individual identity.

1.7 Vision – Mission – Ambition – Role

Research with Success Factor Modeling indicates that the highest levels of performance of an individual, team or organization occur when the levels of success factors related to both ego (ambition and role) and soul (vision and mission) are balanced, aligned and connected to passion.

Passion can be defined as "an intense desire or enthusiasm for something." All successful people and teams have a strong passion for what they are doing.

Your **vision** and your **mission** provide a sense, direction and purpose for expressing your passion.

Your **ambition** directs your desire/will to grow, accomplish, achieve and to benefit and be recognized for those achievements.

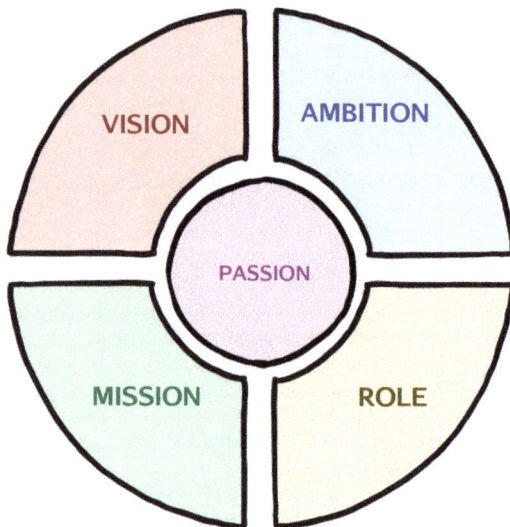

Your **role** defines the position, status and the supporting capabilities and skills, necessary to reach your vision, mission and ambition.

1.8 Modeling

Webster's Dictionary defines a model as "a simplified description of a complex entity or process" such as a "computer model" of the circulatory or respiratory systems. According to the Larousse dictionary, a model is "what is given to serve as a reference, a pattern". The term comes from the Latin root *modus*, which means "way of making or being; method, form, mode, custom, fashion or style. " More specifically, the word "model" is derived from the Latin *modulus* which usually means a "small" version of the original mode. A "model" of an object, for instance, is typically a miniature version or representation of that object. A "working model" (such as that of a machine) is something which can do on a small scale the work that the machine itself does, or is expected to do.

The notion of a "model" has also come to mean "a description or analogy used to help visualize something that cannot be directly observed (an atom, for example)." It can also be used to indicate "a system of postulates, data and inferences presented as a formal description of an entity or situation."

Neuro-Linguistic Programming (NLP) has developed through the modeling of behaviors and processes of human thought. *Modeling behavioral skills* involves observing and mapping the crucial personal and interpersonal processes that produce a successful or remarkable performance of some type. The goal of the behavioral modeling process is to identify the essence of the cognitive elements and actions to be carried out by an individual or group to produce a desired response or outcome – i.e., discovering what is "*the difference that makes the difference*". The process involves breaking a complex performance or interaction into small enough chunks that it can be easily learned by anyone. The purpose of behavior modeling is to create a "model" or a map of a pattern of behavior which can be used to reproduce some aspect of that performance by anyone who is motivated to do so.

Modeling can be likened to identifying the particular key needed to unlock the door to success for various life situations. The "key" corresponding to a specific "lock" is represented by an appropriate combination of behaviors and the related properties of mindset, which are required to effectively address the issues and constraints presented by a certain context.

The objective of the modeling process is not to claim the "correct" or "true" description of the success factors applied by a specific person or group, but rather to create an *instrumental map* (supported by a variety of exercises, formats and tools) that allows individuals or groups to apply the factors that have been modeled in order to achieve key outcomes. Thus, the key criterion for modeling is its **usefulness**.

Expanding upon NLP, the Success Factor Modeling Methodology (SFM™) has been developed to identify, understand and apply the key factors that drive and support successful people, teams and organizations. It is founded upon a set of principles and distinctions which are uniquely suited to analyze and identify crucial trends of *business practices* and *behavioral skills* of successful individuals, teams and companies.

1.9 Scorecards as a modeling tool

To support its modeling "mission", SFM has developed a series of tools to help to assess and foster key success factors in groups and individuals. One such tool is a "Scorecard."

A scorecard can be defined as a table containing the main key factors for the success of a group or team related to the achievement of a particular goal. A scale ranging between the lower level of a particular factor and the higher level helps the group to clarify its level of interaction and to determine areas for improvement. These scorecards can be established for each different level of the pyramid of the logical levels (see page 14).

Example of a scorecard :

Success Factor	Low Level	1+1= -1	1+1= 0	1+1= 1	1+1= 2	1+1= 3	High level
1. Purpose of the project	Ambiguous	1	2	3	4	5	Clear
2. Discussion	Circumspect	1	2	3	4	5	Open
3. Interaction	Avoided	1	2	3	4	5	Engaged
4. Support	Only oneself	1	2	3	4	5	From each to all
5. Use of talents	Poor	1	2	3	4	5 .	Full
6. Rapport	Low	1	2	3	4	5	High
7. Pace	Slow	1	2	3	4	5	Rapid

1.10 Framing

A "framework" refers to the context and the rules that have been collectively established at the formation of a group and within which the group members will work.

The objective of a framework is to ensure that all members of the group are attuned with respect to their common intention as well as to the roles and responsibilities of everyone in the group. It is about setting the conditions to foster a climate of trust and a mindset of partnership. Its purpose is to encourage everyone to listen to one another respectfully and carefully and to provide a structure that helps group members to refocus if they get off track.

1.11 Dynamic Teaming and revolving leadership

Success in today's business environment is increasingly dependent on effective "teamwork". In a challenging and changing environment, effective teamwork requires implementing the principles and skills of "dynamic teaming".

A team can be fundamentally defined as "a group of people working together on a task or uniting their efforts toward the same purpose". Thus, a team can be considered as a group of people gathering to "pull" in the same direction, which produces a generative effect for each team member, and for the entire team.

Dynamic teaming involves the ongoing integration of different competencies and personal traits in a way that each team member is clear about the purpose, roles and responsibilities and operating principles of the team. One naturally occurring example and allegory for "dynamic teaming" is the migration of geese. Some species of geese fly more than 8 000 kilometers annually, between Arctic North American and Central America, at speeds of 80 km/h or more. It is these bird's capacity for dynamic teaming that makes this exceptional feat possible. The lessons we can learn from geese to work dynamically in a team are as follows:

Lesson 1

Fact: As each goose flaps its wings, it creates an "updraft" for the birds behind it. When a goose is able to position itself in the right location behind the flock mate in front of it, it is able to ride on the energy produced by the one ahead, requiring less effort. By flying In a 'V ' formation, the geese add 71 % greater flying range than if each bird flew alone.

Lesson: People who share a common direction and sense of community can get where there are going more quickly and easily because they are traveling on one another's inspiration and energy.

Lesson 2

Fact: When a goose falls out of formation, it suddenly feels the drag and resistance of flying alone.

Lesson: If we have as much sense as a goose, we stay in formation with those headed where we want to go.

Lesson 3

Fact: When the lead bird tires, it rotates back into the formation to take advantage of the lifting power of the bird immediately in front of it.

Lesson: There is an advantage to take turns doing the hard tasks and sharing leadership.

Lesson 4

Fact: The geese flying in formation honk to encourage those in front to keep up their speed.

Lesson: We need to make sure our honking is encouraging. In groups where there is encouragement, productivity is much greater. The power of encouragement (to stand by one's heart or core values and to encourage the heart and core values of others) is the quality of honking that we seek.

Lesson 5

Fact: When a goose gets sick, wounded, or shot down, two geese drop out of formation and follow it down to help and protect it. They stay with it until it dies or is able to fly again. Then, they join another formation or catch up with the flock.

Lesson: If we have as much sense of geese, we will stand by each other in difficult times as well as when we're strong.

1.12 Meetings with Delegated Functions (Réunions déléguées®)

Meetings are one of the most common contexts requiring collective intelligence. Their frequency and organization are key elements for fostering resonance, synergy and emergence, which require the achievement and maintenance of certain types of interactions and ongoing feedback. Of course, what is covered and how the meeting is structured will determine a lot about how much resonance, synergy, emergence, collective intelligence and generative collaboration occur. Without an effective meeting format, as many of us have no doubt experienced, meetings can be a chaotic and ineffective waste of time.

A good example of an effective structure for managing an effective meeting that we recommend looking into is that of Meetings with Delegated Functions. This delegation of functions process, "Delegated meetings" (Réunions Déléguée®), was developed by Alain Cardon, French Master Coach certified by the International Coach Federation since 2002: http://www.metasysteme-coaching.eu/english/. He is also a consultant, trainer, teacher lecturer, author and co-author of more than fifteen books in the fields of management and human resources.

Similar to the "lessons from geese" presented on the previous pages, the Meeting with Delegated Functions format allows the leader of a group or team to share different roles (the facilitator, the decisions driver, the scribe, the pace keeper/time keeper, the observer or meta person, etc.) with the participants. By doing so, we move from a meeting where the functions are centralized to a meeting that, like a flock of geese, allows for the development of collective performance.

Chapter 2

Our Approach

Our interest in developing the PERICEO project came from our own experiences working in teams, companies and organizations. Our goal was to apply our own collective intelligence to create a pragmatic research project that would identify the key success factors supporting the emergence of collective intelligence in teams and organizations.

To present the sequence of events that resulted in the development of the PERICEO Tool, we have chosen to follow the "imagineering" process developed by Walt Disney. The term is a combination of "imagination" and "engineering". The process of imagineering is structured around the balance and coordination of three fundamental mindsets: dreamer, realist and critic.

> *"To realize something really extraordinary, you have to begin by dreaming about it. Then, wake up calmly and go to the end of your dream. Never give up."*
>
> Walt Disney.

Walt Disney has become a myth, a legend ... He has made millions of people dream around the world; both children and adults! He has always been, and still is, considered a major reference point for innovation and creativity in an organizational context.

Throughout his career, Robert Dilts has "modeled" the strategies applied by various geniuses such as Walt Disney, Mozart, Leonardo de Vinci, Aristotle, Tesla, Freud and many others. His goal in doing so is to highlight how these people think and what they do, specifically, to achieve such a degree of success and achievement.

According to Robert, Walt Disney had an original and very effective creative strategy that involved moving through three different mindsets: Dreamer, Realist and Critic. Disney optimized this process by dedicating a specific workspace to the Dreamer, another one to the Realist, and a third one to the Critic. This helped him to make sure to keep a balance between the three modes of approaching something.

If we remain only in the Dreamer mindset, we are not likely to ever achieve very much. Similarly, a Realist, without a Dreamer and a Critic is just a robot, constantly executing but with no real direction or feedback. A Critic on its own is simply a killer or spoiler. A Dreamer and Realist make a lot of prototypes but rarely reach a level of quality and sustainability to create something that lasts. A Realist and Critic are essentially a bureaucracy, restricted to preserving only what already exists. A Dreamer and Critic produce a "bi-polar" interaction that gets lost in a never-ending conflict.

So, how do we concretely implement the Disney strategy?

1. Generate new ideas through 'Dreamer' qualities.

2. Pragmatically structure these ideas through 'Realist' qualities.

3. Consider possible obstacles or difficulties through the 'Critic' position.

When working with a team, it is helpful, if possible, to dedicate a different room for each of these mindsets, or at least a different space within the same room.

The Dreamer

"The future looks big and glittering" — Walt Disney

The quote above characterizes the Dreamer attitude. It was Disney's answer when asked about his vision for his company just after the release of his classic film, and first big international success, *Snow White*.

Disney's Dreaming room had pictures all over the walls. In this room, the team created a comprehensive vision of the project, without any concern yet about how that vision would be implemented. Imagination is what is most crucial at this stage. However, it is important to explore the dream through all of the possible sensory channels: visual, auditory, somatic ...

The Dreamer focuses on **what** is possible*?*

This stage seeks to answer questions such as:

* What is the vision?
* What is possible?
* What is the longer-term aim of the project?
* What benefits will the project bring to you and others?
* What other possibilities could it lead to in the future?
* By developing this project, who and what do you want to become?

The Realist

The Realist phase focuses on **how** the dream is to be implemented?

The goal of the Realist stage is to create a concrete action plan, a "storyboard" to define the key steps and the sequence of those steps, with the corresponding timing. Rationality and logic are critical at this stage.

The Realist seeks to answer questions such as:

* How, specifically, will you implement your vision?
* What resources do you need?
* What people do you need?
* How are you going to proceed?
* What are the specific steps?

The Critic

"Put your work twenty times upon the anvil"

Nicolas Boileau

The Critic phase focuses on **why** we are doing something a certain way?

The aim of the Critic stage is to identify missing links and possible sources of error.

The questions to be asked include:

* Who could be positively or negatively impacted by the project?

* Why could someone object to the project? What are their needs or expectations?

* What is missing?

* Under what circumstances would you not carry out this project?

A good Critic will put himself or herself in the point of view of all potential stakeholders.

We intentionally and explicitly followed each stage of Disney's Imagineering process as we pursued our collaboration for the PERICEO project.

2.1 The Dreamer

Inspired by Martin Luther King ... We have a dream.

We dream of a better world where all people are born not only free and equal in rights, but also where each person is responsible for his or her own growth and personal development as well as the growth and thriving of the collective.

We dream of a world where financial profits are distributed appropriately to all of the key players, not just selectively shared by only a few people.

In the words of Albert Einstein, we dream of a society that nourishes the needs and desires of each person while creating a virtuous circle or feedback loop supporting each one of us to contribute to create a better world for everyone

Our dream, our vision* is of a society to which each of us wishes to belong...

... We are consultants,coaches, trainers and business professionals, so let us begin to dream actively!

Our mission*: To discover precisely HOW we can contribute to generate a "difference that makes a difference" through collective intelligence.

We all recognize contexts and situations in organizations "that work", i.e., where "1 + 1 ≥ 3". Shouldn't it be possible to identify and show what happens differently in these situations? To create a model and duplicate it in situations where it is desperately needed? Because excellence can be modeled, why do we deprive ourselves of it? By creating a model that would permit us to evaluate the level of Collective Intelligence in any group or organization – public companies, private associations, educational institutions and in NGO's – we could help to infuse this way of thinking and operating at all levels of society! **We could help new, ecological systems to emerge; systems that raise the level of consciousness of individuals and collectives. How? By training, writing, facilitating, supervising, transmitting through conferences worldwide! Wouldn't that be wonderful?**

Our dream began in 2013...during the three-year training program to become Facilitators in Collective Intelligence, given by Robert Dilts in Avignon, France, that started in April, 2012. Study and research groups were one of the unique aspects of this training. The context was an ideal one for offering participants (professionals in organizations) to become involved in this dream of how to foster Collective Intelligence in teams and organizations. On October 21st, 2013, at one of the meetings of the training group, Robert introduced the idea that inspired PERICEO: Projet d'Etude et de Recherche de l'Intelligence Collective dans les Entreprises et les Organisations (Project to Study the of Role of Collective Intelligence in Companies and Organizations). He offered, to those who wanted, to join this learning project and take it to another level by forming a study group, composed of co-player and co-modeler roles* with him and Gilles Roy as supervisors.

The aims of the study, our ambition*:

The group established the following goals as the ambition of the study:

* Awaken awareness and interest in Collective Intelligence and promote the expertise of Dilts Strategy Group (DSG) among target businesses.

* Establish personal contacts with interviewees.

* Publish the results of the study in targeted media.

* Create openings and opportunities for others.

* Test the resulting tools and models with potential customers.

2.2 The Realist

There were two important aspects relating to the Realist phase of the project: *form* (how we worked together on the project) and *substance* (the content of our study).

For the first aspect, we decided to apply the principles and practices of Collective Intelligence that we were learning in the training to our own interactions. We operated according to some basic principles of Collective Intelligence, namely:

The use of revolving leadership*: depending on the phases of the project, different people emerged as leaders.

* Stage 1: Creation and editing of the questionnaire and conducting interviews with representatives of selected companies

* Stage 2: Collaboratively developing the assessment tool based on the interview results

* Stage 3: Applying and refining the tool through giving feedback to the participating organizations

* Stage 4: Transmitting the results through writing and training.

* It is interesting to note that, for the most time consuming phase of the project, it was through sharing leadership that the group was able to maintain its energy and commitment. This in itself is a model of "rotating leadership"; which we will come back to later on.

* Similarly, it is important to note that it was only when our meetings (scheduled teleconferences) were planned ahead of time that the work progressed efficiently. This validated the importance of keeping to a consistent rhythm and framework.

* At each of our meetings, usually held as conference calls, the roles* of facilitator, time-keeper and decision initiator alternated among the group participants (as "delegated functions"). This brought about increased co-responsibility and performance within the group.

* Meetings were held at a regular pace, along with work between sessions and respect for the commitments made between these sessions. Large group meetings were scheduled on a quarterly basis to ensure that the sub-groups maintained their connection and rapport and kept up with each other's progress, along with meetings in self-managed subgroups on a monthly or even weekly basis

* Implementation of a collaborative tool: we adopted a Dropbox folder that everyone could add to or consult, depending on the timing of the project and the ongoing tasks. (For example, during interviews, this enabled us to collect and consult information; when setting up calendars or summaries, everyone could consult all work in progress). The Dropbox folder was also available to working groups of subsequent training sessions (e.g., in metropolitan France as well as in French overseas departments and regions - Réunion Island - and in the USA - Santa Cruz) to review and refer to previous stages.

* We maintained certain principles used by Open Space Technology, notably *"The people who show up are the right people"*: the number of people involved in this project varied depending on periods, from 25 at the beginning to 6-7 at other times, then 4 at the last stage, and this allowed for a fluid process where each group member was able to undertake a task at a chosen moment rather than just being present.

a. The Organization

Concretely, we needed to formulate a tool and a work method that allowed us to demonstrate, and if possible measure, the presence of collective intelligence within teams, regardless of which company or team was involved.

This required that we discover and model exactly how the high performing teams and companies generate and activate collective intelligence. We accomplished this by applying principles learned during our first two training sessions and by elaborating strategies in order to develop and enhance our own observations and modeling processes.

The project 1) involved working with companies and organizations, 2) resonated with our previous professional experience, and 3) seemed realistic to us. We also saw it as a chance to actively interact with businesses as actors, ambassadors and coaches for Collective Intelligence while still learning-by-doing. All of this was very motivating for us.

We thought it was important that each of us, as an "I serving a WE," contributed to the creation of a vision of the world to which we wanted to belong. Our intention was to put the concepts of holons and holarchies* into practice through the project. We assumed that each one of us was a complete and independent whole and at the same time a part of successively larger "wholes" that included and transcended us: i.e., our PERICEO group and our business partners, but also our families and friends, our respective work communities.

During the training, we also learned the importance of being fully present in relation to oneself and others. Thus, another key intention* for the project was to safeguard this "presence", to work toward accepting each of us with no misunderstanding, and to ensure that each of us could establish and maintain rapport and have constructive relationships and interactions with other project members; i.e., to consistently practice the COACH State*.

The experience, as you will see later, would make us realize that the leap from theory to practice is not always a comfortable one. It was, however, an enriching and significant learning experience; one that strengthened our appreciation for equanimity and accountability among ourselves, with the PERICEO group and with our business partners.

b. The Working Community

Because we wanted to create a very pragmatic tool, and since groups and teams may demonstrate characteristics of Collective Intelligence in some contexts and not others, it seemed logical to us to meet directly with these teams and organizations and interview them in their own environment. Therefore, our group decided to operate as a research unit with the intention to gather as much information as possible through interviews conducted "in the field" and then identify the common factors that were most relevant in order to build our model.

The first step involved presenting the research project to all the participants in the Collective Intelligence training program to see how many of them would be interested in getting involved in a work of this magnitude. We wanted to have as many participants in the project as possible. Twenty-five members of the group joined us. Approximately a third of the group.

The size and geographical spread of the project group was both a great asset and a major challenge. The group members were all professionally active, with many other professional commitments. In addition, geographically speaking, the group was "all over the map" (participants from different regions of France, Belgium and Switzerland). This reality meant that we had to adjust our agendas and communicate and interact mainly using digital means through conference calls (where the sound quality was not always so good), emails and Dropbox.

Benefits:

* We kept track of our progress through the written reports of telephone conferences and through e-mails. All important information was recorded and saved in the shared Dropbox folder. This was an opportunity for us to be explicit, precise in our communications, and creative. Moreover, this style of communicating would play a fundamental part in the emergence of our tool!

* We became aware of the strengths and weaknesses of the collaborative tools (see page 46).

* Rigor and discipline were time savers.

* And, of course, the diversity of the selected organizations (size, business context, activity) was in itself a source of enrichment! (See the "The Selection Process" on pages 33-34.)

Disadvantages:

* Non verbal communication could not be studied or evaluated on the phone or for communication in writing.

* Information could not be accessed when telephone or Internet connections were disrupted or cut off!

* At certain key moments of our progress, we needed to meet IRL (in real life). In this context, "physical" contact was crucial.

We also think it is important to highlight that at every meeting, be they virtual or IRL, we made sure to create the conditions required for generative collaboration: to start the meeting with a COACH state*, to repeat the COACH state exercise at times of confusion or scattering, and establish a shared framework. This has enabled us to remain connected and to mobilize all our resources. At the end of the meeting, we also made sure to define the next step before concluding by using a word, a metaphor or a gesture (especially for IRL meetings).

c. The selection process

The businesses we selected to study represented:

* Different sectors of activity (in the public or private spheres)
    - Industry, Services, Technology, Environment, Collective, Education.

* Various Company Sizes and Business Profiles
    - ≤ 50 persons, ≤ 250 persons, > 250 persons.
    - SMEs, subsidiaries or teams from large companies or multinationals, etc.

* Various Business Phases
    - Growth, Expansion, Maturity.

* Variety in Reputation and Recognition
    - Peer recognition, local, regional, national or international recognition.

The respondents had diverse profiles and cultural differences:

* Top managers, middle managers
  - Assessed at the onset.

* Collaborators, teams
  - Assessed at a later date to validate key factors of Collective Intelligence.

The four mandatory criteria of interviewee selection included:

* An innovative managerial mode rewarding cooperation (Collective Intelligence or generative collaboration).

* More than 15 people in the team or organization.

* Economically viable business (financially stable, if not growing).

* Win-win relationships with our business partners (see Appendix 4, " Charter and the Code of Ethics or the PERICEO project').

The research group contacted various teams and companies asking if they were willing to take part in the required exchanges and interviews lasting from one hour to several days.

Ultimately, 22 companies corresponding to the profile were selected for the interviews. They were considered partners and stakeholders in the PERICEO adventure.

d. Putting the study into practice: Climbing the "Collaboration Spiral."

" *None of us, acting alone, can achieve success!*"
– Nelson Mandela

"*To do great things, you must not stand above men, you must stand with them. *" – Montesquieu

During our collective intelligence training, we discovered that the mindset of generative collaboration is about team synergy in order to make the "whole pie bigger." The key to success in this case was connectivity.

* Collaboration enabled us to increase our range of influence in order to fulfill our mission and achieve our vision.

* Relationships with key individuals formed the networks that led to the next level of performance and achievement.

* Each new level was accompanied by a corresponding expansion of identity.

This corresponded to what is known as a "collaboration spiral" (*SFM Vol II: Generative Collaboration*, pp. 218-229). The diagram on the following page illustrates the progression of the PERICEO group's actors and their level of progress at each stage of the project: an upward spiral in which each loop represents a different stage of the project as it unfolded and expanded in an "organic" way.

The group continued to function, applying the principle of rotating leadership, with all leaders serving the PERICEO vision. One of the key factors of Collective Intelligence is having exemplary role models, starting with the leaders. Gilles Roy and Robert Dilts, as well as the various PERICEO leaders, embodied the mindset underlying generative collaboration.

Gilles and Robert (with the support of Deborah Bacon Dilts) were indeed very present in phases 1 and 2. Then they moved more to the side – always present and supporting, intervening as "guides" during transitions from one stage to another, or in the event of a need expressed by the group members. Similarly, other project group members – according to their desire, energy, skills and agenda – volunteered and committed themselves as group leaders and / or sub-group leaders for one or another stage of the project before returning back to a contributor role. This is how the group matured in autonomy and empowerment, as did each individual member, in order to achieve PERICEO's ambition* and fulfill its mission while serving the vision*.

Group Vision: A world to
which we are proud to belong.

Vision
We

- Step 8 (to come):
Transmitting the results
to companies and
organizations around the
world

Group Mission: To model Collective Intelligence by applying
Collective Intelligence and to
make it visible and implement it
wherever it may be useful.

Mission

- Step 7: Formulating
conclusions,
communications,
conferences, workshops,
articles, book (10
persons)

November 2016

- Step 6: Giving feedback
/ testing with business
partners, workshops (9
persons)

February 2016

- Step 5: Filtering results,
synthesis, representation
(9 persons pilot phase
- 20 persons then 12
production phase)

July 2015

- Step 4: Gathering of
information, interviews,
transcripts (19 persons)

December 2014

- Step 3: Selecting
business partners &
contacts (22 persons)

March 2014

- Step 2: Determining
methodology (12
persons)

- Step 1: Developing
an action plan, script,
common framework (12
persons)

Key collaborators

- Project launch (22
persons).

21 October 2013

Values / beliefs   **Self**   Mind / purpose

Skills / capabilities   Emotions

Behaviors / strategies

The PERICEO Project Collaboration Spiral

e. The emergence of the tool

> *Without creative, independently thinking and judging personalities, the upward development of society is as unthinkable as the development of the individual personality without the nourishing soil of the community.* – Albert EINSTEIN

As we mentioned in Chapter 1 - Fundamentally, the three pillars of Collective Intelligence are resonance, synergy and emergence. Without going through the first two, there is little chance that something new will "emerge"! And remember, at the beginning of this adventure, we did not really know what we were going to find. We trusted the process, were passionate about the issue, and at the same time we were progressing with uncertainty as to the outcome. It was at Step 5, after all of the information had been gathered and we were filtering the results that the tool emerged!

Before continuing, we want to say something important about the conditions for emergence. As an example, this book has been collectively written by four people: Isabelle, Elisabeth, Gilles and Robert. While each of us may have been more active in the drafting of one or another part of it, we have all systematically re-read and commented on the whole work and made edits or changes. We know that, for the process of Collective Intelligence to work, the individual is as important as the collective. Often, what happens at times of emergence is that it comes through one person, although necessarily resulting from all the interactions between the members of the group. To illustrate this, here is the testimony of Elisabeth, who experienced this emergence regarding the tool, followed by that of Isabelle, who was the first to interact with her after it happened.

Elisabeth Falcone

> *Emergence often takes place after a CRASH. This had been essentially a theory for me, until this point in the project. The theory, however, was about to become a concrete experience.*
>
> *As part of the usual monthly review organized for several months, I had scheduled a conference call one evening with some of my colleagues from the project. At the expected time, I logged into the system to open the meeting at 7:30PM. Pleasant background music began to play, 5 minutes, 10 minutes passed, then 15 ... and no one else joined the call. Already logged on my computer, I had at least the opportunity to view our various files, reports, summaries, etc. At this stage of the project, we had explored and used the recorded interviews, worked on the key factors which were organized according to logical levels*.*

Time kept passing and there was still no contact from anyone. In thinking back over the moment, between my state of fatigue and the music I must have been at that time in a sort of COACH* state, or at least in a kind of emotional letting go state, while eyeing the files for several minutes more.

However, after about half an hour of waiting, I logged out a bit annoyed. I decided it was better to express this CRASH* in order to let it go and sent an email to my colleagues, roughly saying, 'I appreciate and value each of you but what just happened now is not O.K.for me. You might be busy and tired. I am too. I would have appreciated a sign from you saying that you could not attend.' And I left my office with only one thought in mind: Relax and enjoy my evening. And while I was letting go for a few minutes, I literally 'saw' the tool taking form with the factors grouping themselves into levels to form a sort of colored 'canvas'. Those using Excel and radar graphics will immediately figure out the kind of representation I am talking about (see part III - The Tool). And at that moment I felt such joy, such energy and an irresistible desire to share this experience with my colleagues. Because it was indeed an emergence, which had come through me but at the same time that connected us all, belonging to all of us.

At that moment, I felt that I had to create this tool with my hands. I didn't immediately think of Excel and its radar graphics; rather, I grabbed colored pencils and drew quickly what I had in mind. Also, I wanted – or rather needed – to communicate with someone. I began by calling Isabelle then I called other colleagues (including some of those who didn't join the scheduled conference call, because, in the end it was thanks to them that I experienced that moment, isn't it?). I sent them a scan of my illustration by email. The message was: "Look I have just thought about this, what do you think?' There were several very positive responses the very next day, it resonated with several of them ... and we continued to follow in that path. The next step was to transfer the representation to Excel which we will discuss later, along with the organizing of the key factors grouped into a Scorecard*.

A number of points seem to me to characterize this experience:

- *The centered and non-attached state I was in when I was reviewing the files with the light, pleasant music echoing in my ears.*
- *The letting go moment I had prior to the emergence: 'Drop the thought'.*
- *Verbalizing and sharing the "CRASH".*
- *The great sense of joy and rise in energy when I 'saw' the representation. The fatigue vanished.*
- *The irresistible urge to create something with my hands and to share it.*

And of course, the very next morning, I shared with my friend and co-leader Isabelle.

Isabelle Meiss

Since the beginning of this adventure as co-leaders, (June, 2014), Elisabeth and I have got to know each other and learned to work in synergy. At this stage of the adventure in April, 2015, as Elisabeth mentioned above, we had been working in sub-groups for several months synthesizing key factors by level. We kept each other regularly informed on the group's progress in order to keep attuned, which allowed us to move forward on a step-by-step basis. Despite some fatigue, I stayed the course and maintained my focus and passion for this collaborative project. One evening, at the end of a busy work day, I discovered with surprise an email from Elisabeth marked "HELP", asking if she could call me the next day to talk. It was the first time since the beginning of our collaboration that she opened up to me as sincerely about a personal difficulty she was having. Until then, I assumed that Elisabeth was strong and self-assured. I was surprised and touched by, what was for me, a show of trust on her part.

Even though I was a bit frustrated about how slowly the project was advancing, the weather was mild and I was calm and feeling in a resource state in front of my computer screen, self-confident and full of energy. In addition, the meetings with my sub-groups had gone well and had been productive. I felt in a position to welcome Elisabeth's news, to step into her perspective, to check my agenda and to propose that she call me the following afternoon.

The next day, still unaware of Elisabeth's difficulties and feeling fine, I calmly prepared for our phone call. My intention* was to listen to her and to contribute, as best as I could, to bring out a solution from our exchange, keeping the connection to the PERICEO vision and mission. It didn`t occur to me at the moment but I think I was in a COACH.* state. I had the pleasant surprise to hear Elisabeth's playful voice and what she told me made me even happier. The night before she had had an enlightening "breakthrough" and saw what was missing...: an overall representation of the work of recent months, she could translate it through a drawing she made.

What she described resonated* within me and I realized that we were entering into a new phase of the project. Following this enjoyable moment of sharing, we spoke about the next step. It just so happened that a conference call of the entire PERICEO team had been scheduled a few days later to discuss the progress. Elisabeth wanted to share her breakthrough with the group and her plan was to use Excel to enrich her drawing, but she worried that she would not have the time to do it by the meeting. An idea occurred to me...when emailing the meeting invitation why not announce her breakthrough to everyone by including it as one topics on the agenda? I suggested that we attach to the invitation a scan of the drawing with her comments and ask for feedback from everyone, trusting that It might energize the group and could become a generative opportunity... one of the learning points taken from our training, and yet another chance to practice! She sent off the email to the whole group. Her model was a big hit and the following pages describe the rest of the story.

In conclusion

The actual operation of the tool is presented in Part III. What is important for us here is to show the process as a whole and the phenomenon of emergence when all the conditions are fulfilled. The time taken to establish a solid relationship, to build the framework, to capitalize on our differences, to undertake tasks and commit to the responsibilities involved, to maintain the rhythm of the project and have quality interactions, led to this gratifying phase of emergence! Being comfortable with uncertainty by having a clear passion-driven Vision*, can truly bring us to living the reality of generative collaboration.

2.3 The Critic

Once our model had been established, we needed to assess its relevance, to determine its impact and usefulness, and to identify the potential objections, improvements and readjustments to be made. To accomplish this, we began to test our model with different audiences.

a. Feedback and Constructive Criticism from Business Partners

We first returned to the companies that we had interviewed to get feedback on the tool (that had emerged as described in the previous pages). We always started with a one-to-one meeting with the executives who were are point of contact. Some of them, convinced of the value of the PERICEO tool, wanted to test it immediately with their teams. The following are examples of the feedback we received.

> The exercise helped me to take a step back, made me think, and realize what are the important things to do this year: to put technical innovation aside temporarily and work on HR organization, to redefine who we are, what we are doing and for what purpose, to work together on the vision and make it even more of a 'dream carrier and source of action'. My first step will be to use this at a meeting and in our next newsletter.

> 'Again I have been working with a very busy schedule these last weeks. I am going to slow down and refocus on my collaborators. I feel they need me.'

- Examples of what emerged during a working day involving executives and teams

Once feedback was given and adjustments were made with the executives of the business partner companies, we incorporated the tool as part of a workshop for the companies' teams. By applying the tool in their working environment, the teams were able to:

1. **Collectively assess, for each level of success factors, their strengths and their path for development based on each team member's perception.**

   The following three photos give you an idea of a collaborative work by all employees of an SME based on the Scorecards of the PERICEO success factors for the first three levels (Vision / Purpose, Identity, Values and Beliefs).

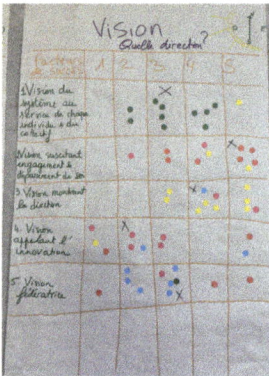

Evaluation of success factors for Purpose / Vision   *Evaluation of Identity level Success Factors*   *Evaluation of Beliefs and Values Success Factors*

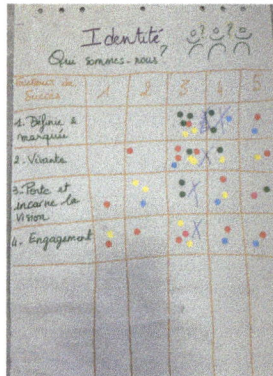

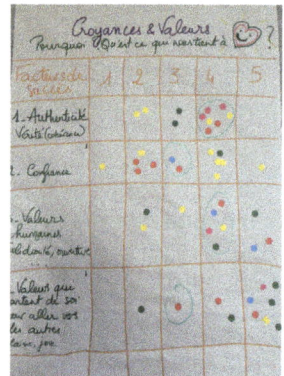

Examples of Scorecards on the PERICEO model made collectively at a seminar day of all employees from a partner company.

2. Collectively determine improvements and actions to be implemented for the future:

We have included in the table below some extracts from what the employees produced together and which emerged following the evaluations.

Examples of improvements to work on	Practical examples of actions
• Better knowledge and understanding of each service. • Interactions: greater acknowledgment of the needs to make decisions, better listening to the expectations and needs of everyone in order to overcome selfishness. • Improving confidence: everyone is trained and skilled. • More communication debriefing and better transfer of knowledge between departments, same level of information for all. • Vision / innovation to simplify and to save time and energy. • Sharing and replicating innovations. • Valuing each individual. • Exemplary and mutual trust. • Moving from words to action	• Free up time off-site and off-work to explore these subjects – "Live my life, not just do my job". • Integration of newcomers. • Be key player in the department. • Organize joint meetings, and inter-service sharing. • Eat together. • Redesign working/meeting spaces.

This first round of feedback from our business partners validated the usefulness of the tool. It also highlighted a need for clarification within the PERICEO facilitators' group, in particular in the formulation of the key factors for vision and identity as well as values and beliefs.

In April 2016,we decided to set up a sub-group to work on this in a collaborative mindset, expressed through constructive criticism. This resulted in:

1. A thorough inventory of the key factors.

2. A revision of the high and low scores of the key factors for each scorecard. Because they emerged from the collective work on the 22 interviews, there was concern that changing them could distort the consistency of the study. The important thing, however, was to agree on statements using the most neutral terms possible.

3. A step-by-step reformulation of high and low scores for vision, identity and values and beliefs levels in particular.

In the end, it was collectively decided to keep the scorecards with more neutral reformulations for the high and low values of key factors. The updated model was then presented to a wider audience by some of the members of the PERICEO team at conferences, trainings and customer visits.

b. Feedback and Constructive Criticism from collective workshops

As an example, Isabelle and Elisabeth presented the model at the 4th International Congress of Collective Intelligence, held on 10 November 2016, organized by Vision 2021 and MOM21 at the Palais des Papes in Avignon.[1] the theme was:

"Which leadership abilities foster the emergence of key factors in collective intelligence and ... perpetuate them over time?"

The workshop was moderated by the two co-leaders for a group of about 50 people from the business community with different profiles and aroused a great deal of interest and involvement from group members.

---

1   www.vision-2021.fr/action/2016/07/06/le-congres-de-lintelligence-collective-2016/

For this workshop, participants applied what they had learned to promote generative collaboration among the group members and use their Collective Intelligence to help add to the model.

The table presented below is an example of input from the participants validating the connection between the various levels of success factors associated with collective intelligence and effective leadership. Comments such as these were used to help refine the model further.

Success Factors	Participants' feedback at the end of the workshop
The Vision is ecological for the system, the individual and the collective	*The transmission of Leadership –* *To have a vision and share it with others in order to develop creativity - a collective mindset - Support - Be meaningful: For what? - Provide direction, energize - Take leadership together = co-leadership.*
The Sense of Identity is Alive.	*Accept who you are! - Leader's ethics.*
Beliefs that support each person humanity and are in service of Life (solidarity, openness, accountability ...).	*Respect our values, have self-respect to better respect others - Solidarity, like the geese - Confidence - Authenticity.*
The Capability to evolve together, personally and professionally, for both leaders and team members. **The Capacity** to accept chaos and use it creatively.	*Energy - Resonance (alignment).* *Collective Actions.*
Behavior: Be an example (walk the talk).	*Revolving leadership - to lead by example, caring - goodwill - Connection - to inspire confidence, to give energy, to accompany change, to remove barriers.*
Environment: Diversity and flexibility.	*Collective outcomes.*

2.4 What We Learned from Our Own Collective Work

While the key success factors relating to conditions that foster the emergence of Collective Intelligence were mainly observed in the training setting or when they emerged from the interviews and interventions we had conducted in companies, a number of others became clear as a result of our own collective work as a research team. These included:

* The critical importance of having a clear framework (without a framework, the project did not move forward) and explicitly communicating that framework within the team.

* The importance of having someone take the lead at each stage.

* The importance of co-leading, especially for the longest and most decisive phases.

* The Importance of being aligned at all times with the group vision (if not, there is a lack of motivation to carry out such an intensive amount of work).

* A Corollary: being passionate about a subject determines and reinforces people's commitment over time.

* The collaborative tool is just an extension of the human interactions that already exist. The effectiveness of the tool is enhanced if the interactions are rich and promising, otherwise it is neglected.

* Dynamics within the PERICEO group: such as the pace and the quantity and quality of exchanges were key.

* The PERICEO dynamic collaboration spiral: see diagram p. 29.

It is a distinct pleasure to write this endorsement for Isabelle Meiss and Elisabeth Falcone. Elisabeth and Isabelle are two of the most dedicated, proactive and collaborative people I know. They have committed themselves to bringing the power and magic of Succes Factor Modeling to others through both their teaching and their example.

As co-authors with me and Gilles Roy on the book **The PERICEO Tool for Teams and Organizations: Developing your Capacities for Collective Intelligence**, Isabelle and Elisabeth are by far the most qualified people I know to teach others how to use the collective intelligence assessment tools that have come from the PERICEO modeling project.

I strongly recommend them to teams and companies seeking to increase their productivity and contribution through collective intelligence ."

Robert Dilts - March 2018

« C'est avec un grand plaisir que je rédige ces mots de soutien pour Isabelle Meiss et Elisabeth Falcone. Elisabeth et Isabelle sont deux des personnes les plus dévouées, proactives et collaboratives que je connaisse. Elles se sont engagées à susciter la puissance et la magie de la Modélisation des Facteurs de Succès chez d'autres par leur enseignement et leur exemple.

En tant que co-auteurs avec Gilles Roy de l'ouvrage **L'Outil PERICEO : Équipes et organisations, développer vos capacités d'Intelligence Collective**, Isabelle et Elisabeth sont de loin les personnes les plus qualifiées pour transmettre à d'autres comment utiliser les outils d'évaluation de l'intelligence collective issus du projet de modélisation PERICEO.

Je les recommande fortement aux équipes et aux entreprises cherchant à développer leur productivité et leur contribution par l'intelligence collective. »

Robert Dilts - Mars 2018

Chapter 3

The tool

In this section, we will present the tool that was created as a result of the research we have described in the previous chapters. The tool consists of six scorecards whose purpose is to assess different levels of success factors related to fostering Collective Intelligence in teams and organizations. We want to point out in advance that, in order to help people get the best use of the tool, we have developed a two-day training program that includes specific support for how to apply the tool within an organization. (See appendix A7).

This tool is based on evaluating several different levels of success factors (Dilts pyramid)* in order to answer the following question:

What are the key success factors applied by teams and organizations to promote synergies and develop Collective Intelligence in order to address challenges and make the best use of opportunities in the current economic context? What is the difference that makes the difference in terms of environment, behaviors, capabilities and skills, values and beliefs, identity and vision in the organizations involved?

As a reminder, these levels include:

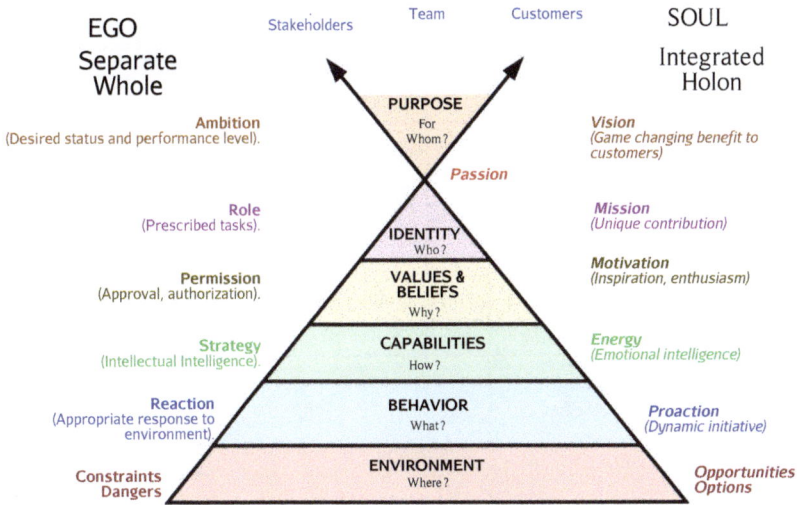

EGO
Separate
Whole

SOUL
Integrated
Holon

Stakeholders Team Customers

PURPOSE
For
Whom?

Passion

Ambition
(Desired status and performance level).

Vision
(Game changing benefit to customers)

Role
(Prescribed tasks).

IDENTITY
Who?

Mission
(Unique contribution)

Permission
(Approval, authorization).

**VALUES &
BELIEFS**
Why?

Motivation
(Inspiration, enthusiasm)

Strategy
(Intellectual Intelligence).

CAPABILITIES
How?

Energy
(Emotional intelligence)

Reaction
(Appropriate response to environment)

BEHAVIOR
What?

Proaction
(Dynamic initiative)

**Constraints
Dangers**

ENVIRONMENT
Where?

**Opportunities
Options**

With regard to modeling, the ideal number of distinctions to be considered for a particular level of success factors is '7 plus-or-minus 2'. (Research has shown that this is the number of items most easily stored and evaluated in short term memory). In developing our tool, we have tried to stay as close as possible to this ideal for each of the levels concerned.

For each level of success factors, we have co-constructed a score-card with statements representing a high level and a low level in order to help managers and their collaborators to respond.

The scores are then represented on a "radar" chart to help highlight strengths and key areas for development.

The six scorecards with example radar charts are presented on the following pages. We have also developed an on line version of this tool. You can find out more about it on our website: http://www.periceo.com

3.1 Key factors for Vision

Success Factor	Low Level	1+1= -1	1+1=- 0	1+1= 1	1+1= 2	1+1= 3	High level
1. The Vision is Ecological for the system, the individuals and the collective.	*The vision ignores either the individual or the collective or both.*	1	2	3	4	5	*The vision is constantly serving individuals AND the collective.*
2. The vision inspires action, commitment and self-improvement.	*No commitment or self-initiative.*	1	2	3	4	5	*Numerous and spontaneous actions and commitments.*
3. The Vision provides a clear direction.	*There is no obvious, shared sense of direction.*	1	2	3	4	5	*The direction is clear and known by all.*
4. The Vision inspires innovation.	*No innovation.*	1	2	3	4	5	*Numerous and regular innovations.*
5. The Vision unites people.	*People think and act as separate individuals.*	1	2	3	4	5	*Team members share a strong sense of connection and common purpose.*

"Radar" representation (with an example):

Key factors for Vision

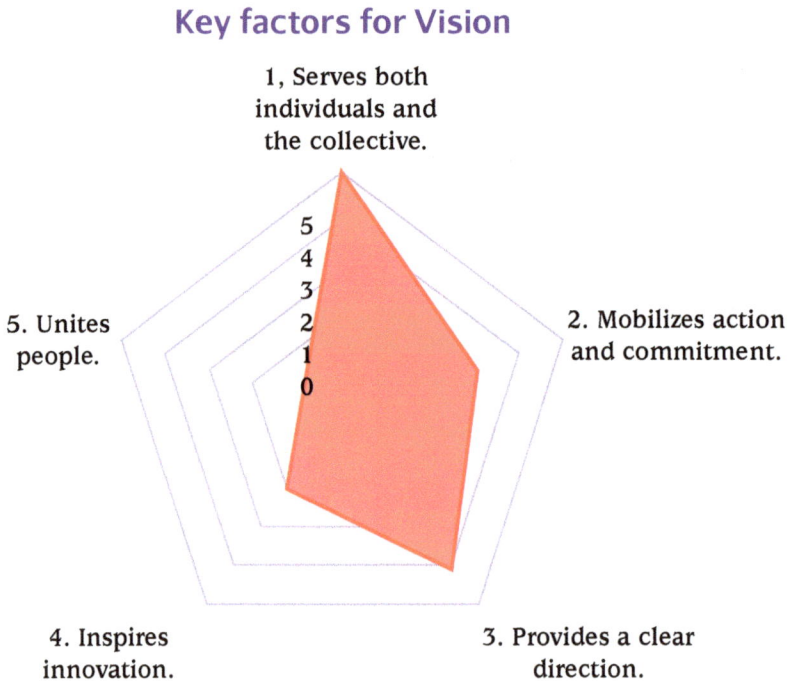

3.2 Key factors for Identity

Success Factor	Low Level	1+1= -1	1+1= 0	1+1= 1	1+1= 2	1+1= 3	High level
1. The collective sense of identity is defined and significant.	*People see themselves as simply knowledgeable performers.*	1	2	3	4	5	*Team members view themselves as conductors, bandmasters and key players in the group's future. Everyone is the guarantor of Collective Intelligence.*
2. The collective sense of identity is alive.	*The group identity is in name only and does not produce interest or energy.*	1	2	3	4	5	*Team members are constantly working together in service of the larger ecosystem.*
3. The collective sense of identity sustains and embodies the Vision (each plays a role in serving the collective identity).	*People are perceived as merely interchangeable professionals.*	1	2	3	4	5	*Team members are concretely involved partners who choose the right role at the right moment (self-organizing).*
4. The collective sense of identity inspires ongoing commitment.	*People make temporary commitments on an individual basis.*	1	2	3	4	5	*Each team member feels a strong ongoing commitment to the larger collective identity.*

"Radar" representation (with an example):

Key factors for Identity

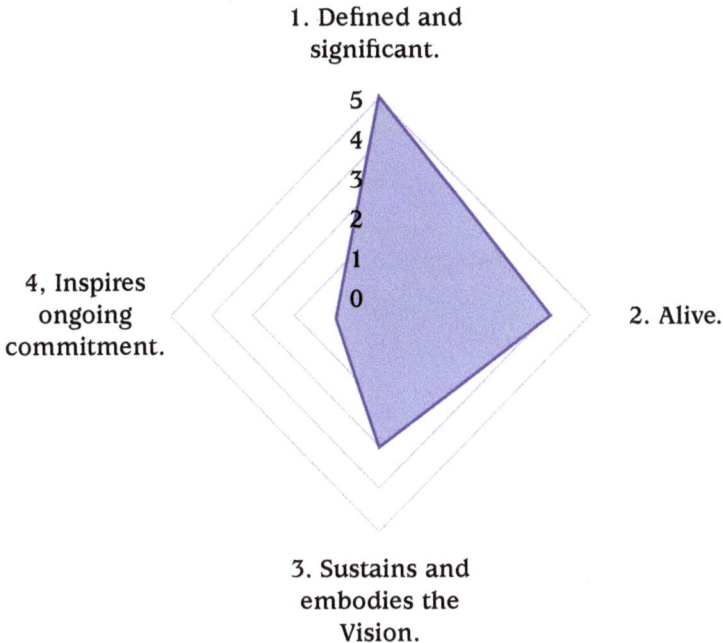

1. Defined and significant.

4, Inspires ongoing commitment.

2. Alive.

3. Sustains and embodies the Vision.

3.3 Key factors for Values and Beliefs

Success Factor	Low Level	1+1= -1	1+1= 0	1+1= 1	1+1= 2	1+1= 3	High level
1. Authentic and truthful.	*People are focused on their own personal interests and not authentic with respect to the collective.*	1	2	3	4	5	*Team members' are aligned and dare to be authentic and truthful with respect to the collective.*
2. Confident in the collective.	*People are confident in themselves or others as individuals.*	1	2	3	4	5	*Team members have a shared confidence in what will eventually emerge from their interactions.*
3. Shared values that support both individuals and the collective (solidarity, openness, responsibility ...).	*People are motivated mostly by values that support their own individual growth and development.*	1	2	3	4	5	*Team members share values that promote the growth and development of both the individual and the larger collective.*
4. Shared beliefs that connect the individual to the collective.	*People believe they should just keep to themselves.*	1	2	3	4	5	*Team members share the belief that their diversity and complementarity create the value of the group.*

"Radar" representation (with an example):

Key factors for Values and Beliefs

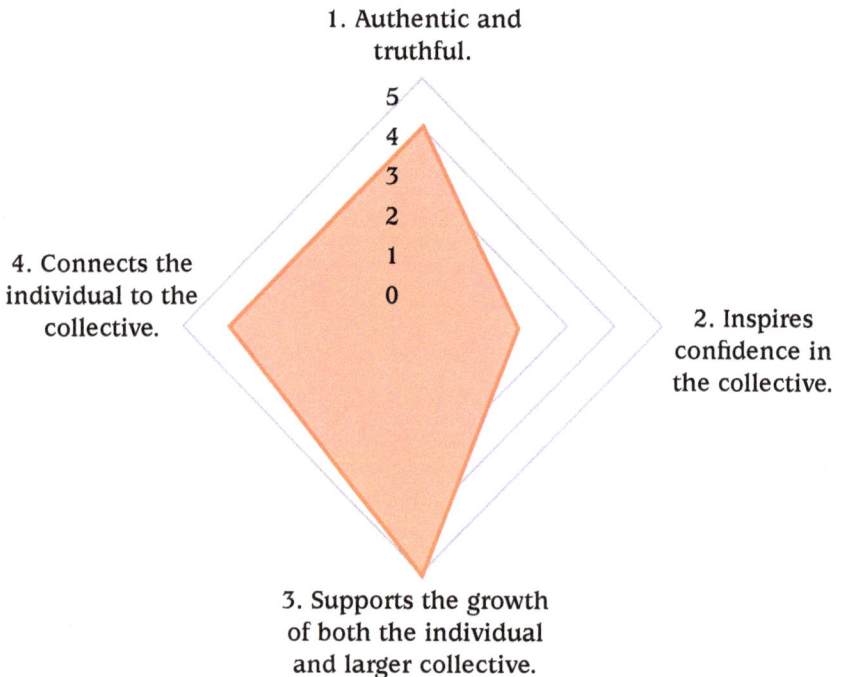

1. Authentic and truthful.

5
4
3
2
1
0

4. Connects the individual to the collective.

2. Inspires confidence in the collective.

3. Supports the growth of both the individual and larger collective.

3.4 key factors for Capabilities

Success Factor	Low Level	1+1=-1	1+1=0	1+1=1	1+1=2	1+1=3	High level
1. To evolve personally and professionally, for both leaders and team members.	*Leaders control and guide the whole process, otherwise nothing happens.*	1	2	3	4	5	*All team members contribute and involve others in a collective transformation.*
2. To contribute to the collective venture while pursuing valuable personal projects.	*People focus only on the projects they have been assigned.*	1	2	3	4	5	*Each team member develops his or her own personal projects while contributing to the projects of others and the company.*
3. To commit oneself and meet commitments.	*Low commitment and reliability.*	1	2	3	4	5	*Team members follow through on their commitments, and support others to do the same.*
4. To demonstrate flexibility and responsiveness to changing conditions- both internally and externally.	*Low responsiveness and flexibility.*	1	2	3	4	5	*Team members are able to adapt quickly to changes in multiple contexts.*
5. To communicate openly and respectfully.	*Everybody is talking but nobody is listening.*	1	2	3	4	5	*Team members value each others' points of view and are able to let go of their own opinions.*
6. To accept chaos and use it creatively.	*Chaos is viewed only as a source of confusion and cacophony.*	1	2	3	4	5	*Team members are able to welcome chaos as an opportunity for the exploration of creative solutions.*

"Radar" representation (with an example):

Key factors for Capabilities

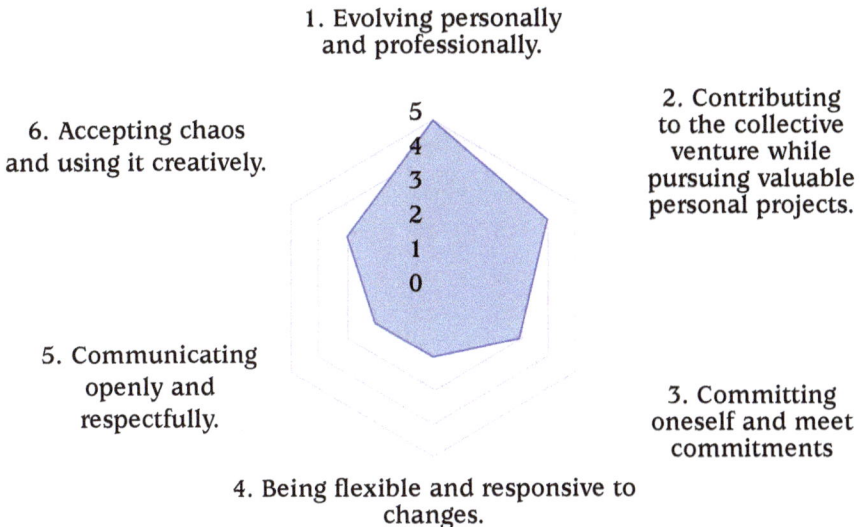

1. Evolving personally and professionally.

6. Accepting chaos and using it creatively.

2. Contributing to the collective venture while pursuing valuable personal projects.

5
4
3
2
1
0

5. Communicating openly and respectfully.

3. Committing oneself and meet commitments

4. Being flexible and responsive to changes.

3.5 Key factors for Behaviors

Success Factor	Low Level	1+1= -1	1+1= 0	1+1= 1	1+1= 2	1+1= 3	High level
1. Numerous and high-quality interactions.	*Periodic short meetings only when necessary to coordinate actions in the same direction.*	1	2	3	4	5	*Numerous and varied interactions with all stakeholders to quickly resolve problems and model excellence.*
2. Positive and realistic attitudes to adversity and complexity.	*Problems trigger reflexive reactions.*	1	2	3	4	5	*The problems lead to the exploration of new opportunities and resources.*
3. Exemplary behavior ("walk the talk").	*Leaders and managers are the only ones who set an example.*	1	2	3	4	5	*All team members strive to set a good example for others.*
4. Constructive use of errors.	*Mistakes are seen as problems and people avoid taking risks.*	1	2	3	4	5	*Risk-taking is encouraged and mistakes are viewed as learning opportunities.*
5. Search for co-construction and collaboration.	*Limited collaboration, done only when necessary.*	1	2	3	4	5	*Everyone is a "servant leader," proactively helping others.*
6. Using the right talent at the right time.	*Individual talents and skills are tolerated but not acknowledged.*	1	2	3	4	5	*Individual talents and skills are recognized as being necessary and valuable.*
7. Promotion of curiosity, exploration and innovation.	*New ways of doing things are only explored when it is absolutely necessary.*	1	2	3	4	5	*Doing things differently is a natural behavior. Team members are always seeking a better way.*

Radar representation (with an example)

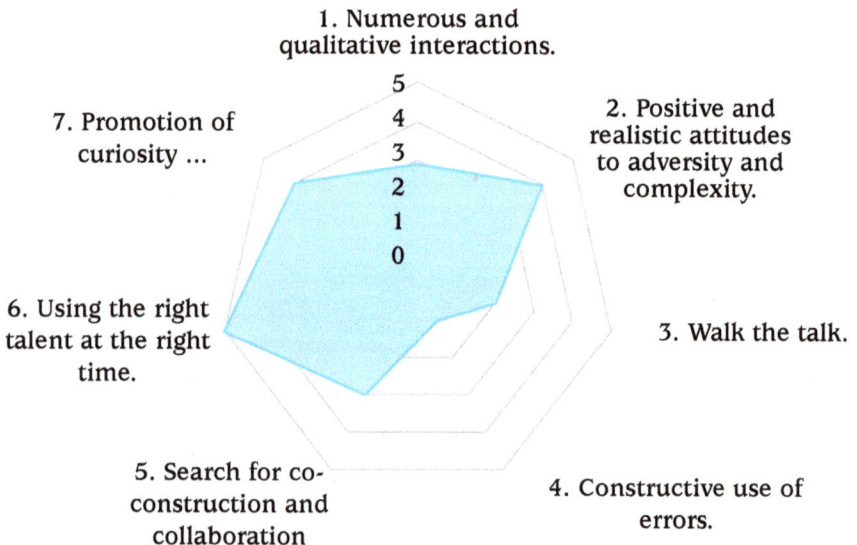

Key factors for Behaviors.

1. Numerous and qualitative interactions.

2. Positive and realistic attitudes to adversity and complexity.

3. Walk the talk.

4. Constructive use of errors.

5. Search for co-construction and collaboration

6. Using the right talent at the right time.

7. Promotion of curiosity ...

3.6 Key factors for Environment

Success Factor	Low Level	1+1= -1	1+1= 0	1+1= 1	1+1= 2	1+1= 3	High level
1. A complex and changing environment is perceived as an asset.	*External pressures are triggers. The collective is only mobilized to answer a specific issue, need or crisis.*	1	2	3	4	5	*Any environmental factor is considered a natural opportunity. Team members adjust constantly.*
2. An open and connected environment to the world.	*Collective Intelligence is linked only to technological innovation (strategic intelligence related to the economy).*	1	2	3	4	5	*Knowledge about the environment comes from multiple human networks (technology is considered just a tool to serve Collective Intelligence).*
3. An environment that promotes diversity and flexibility.	*The teams are homogeneous and keep to themselves.*	1	2	3	4	5	*Teams are naturally diverse and flexible, and key information is shared and available to all.*
4. An environment that allows the change of operating framework.	*People tend to rely on fixed external contexts and resources, such as geographical proximity, standard meeting facilities, IT tools, etc. to provide an operating framework for Collective Intelligence.*	1	2	3	4	5	*The needed framework and resources to create Collective Intelligence is considered to be within each team member, allowing Collective Intelligence to occur at a distance.*

"Radar" representation (with an example):

Key factors for Environment

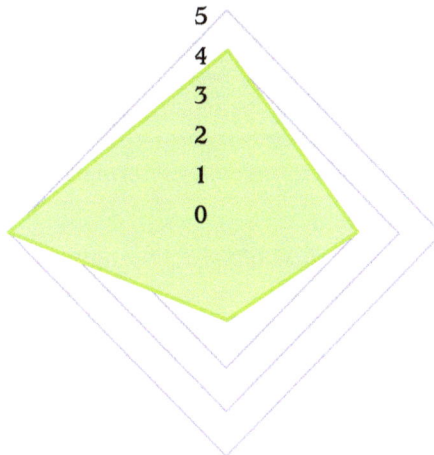

1. Complexity and change are viewed as an asset.

2. Open and connected to the world.

3. Promotes diversity and flexibility.

4. Allows for the change of operating framework.

Conclusion

Our main intention in writing this book has been to share our experience and to support the widest distribution of our tool as possible. Our goal is to help teams and organizations to optimize their capacity for collaboration and to enhance individual awareness.

The PERICEO tool has the advantage of being simple to use and accessible, provided that the basic principles are understood and integrated (see appendix A7). Once you are clear about these basic principles, you will be completely autonomous in applying the scorecards as a diagnostic tool and able to identify areas for improvement and the appropriate actions to take.

Having said that, there is always more to explore and experiment with. Our own journey has led us even further than we envisaged at the time we started this project.

We have experienced time and again what happens during generative collaborations, We know where we are starting, where we want to go, but not necessarily where we will finish! And. by the way, can there really be an end? The end of something is often the beginning of something else!

In any case, you now have in your hands a road map that has multiple applications:

* The description of our collaborative adventure, with its different stages, difficulties and successes provides a structure that you can follow to model any incidents or examples of effective collective performance that you might encounter.

* The description of our creative process – the Disney Strategy or Imagineering process – can be used to effectively facilitate the implementation and increase the effectiveness of a collective project, whatever it is.

* The fundamental principles and practices necessary to foster the process of generative collaboration can be applied to facilitate the emergence of Collective Intelligence in any group or team.

And, of course, there is the tool itself, which, we hope, will inspire you and give you the desire to go further to support your teams - or any group of people with which you are involved - towards more well-being, greater happiness and higher levels of performance, and thus create organizations of a new type.

And now?

One of the strengths of the Success Factor Modeling approach is that it does not actually invent anything new, but simply observes what is already working. Once we know these key success factors, each of us has the capacity to take ownership and apply those "differences that make a difference," both individually and collectively. This can support us to accelerate the development of the awareness and the transformational processes necessary to co-create organizations and social structures based on collaboration, meaning and well-being. Because everything is there, within our reach.

It is up to each individual to choose to make a commitment.

For our part, our commitment is multifaceted:

1. To be at your side and assist you to integrate and use this tool.

2. To conduct different types of seminars and interventions in organizations in order to enable individuals to integrate the soft-skills and know-how necessary to foster Collective Intelligence.

3. To disseminate this work through various conferences and writings: articles, books, blogs, social networks, etc.

4. To conduct a similar study for key factors related to Conscious Leadership and Resilience, and to provide answers to questions such as: when, how, for what reasons can one say of an individual that he or she is acting as a "conscious leader"? And what makes such a person act as a "conscious leader"?

   Why should such a study be carried out? Quite simply because, any time we find true Collective Intelligence, there are necessarily conscious leaders, and vice versa.

If you wish to share your own experiences or thoughts with us, or participate in any way in this adventure; or if you have an idea related to Collective Intelligence or generative collaboration, please contact us! We would be very happy about that.

info@periceo.com
www.periceo.com

Afterword

As we were putting the final touches on this book, we realized how much this journey and our collective work on this publication has transformed us and brought to us on multiple levels.

For both of us, Elisabeth and Isabelle, beyond the revolving leadership that took place during the various phases of this project, our cooperation has been in itself an experience of revolving and interdependent leadership in action as well as a generative collaboration.

We did not know each other before starting the training with Robert Dilts on Collective Intelligence. We had little exchange prior to the beginning of the PERICEO project except about our passion* for diversity. And, while each of us had committed to contribute time and energy to the PERICEO project, we had had little opportunity to work together, since one of us lived in Paris and the other in the south of France. And we were very different personalities!

However, when the time came for a new leader for the PERICEO project to step forward, we both had the desire to take on that role. But it required substantial energy and investment in addition to our professional activities. Neither of us felt that we could take it on alone. We each immediately sensed it would be an adventure for two. That is how we ended up proposing ourselves as "co-pilots."

Today, we realize that "synergy" is not just a word, and we both have the feeling that we have grown together during this journey. Each of us has brought something to the other, How this dynamic unfolded between us is something else that we want to share with you.

First, we successfully tested our ability to be concrete and pragmatic together. If one of us was not able to follow through on a commitment, the other was there to help. At critical times of demotivation, or extra workload, we were able to call the other and talk about it. To be listened to and understood by another person without judgment and with goodwill has been a source of strength that enabled us to collaborate effectively. This included missed appointments: making arrangements for a specific day and time and then canceling it at the last moment with mutual understanding and without taking offense. What has allowed us to continue? A very strong resonance* with the subject of Collective Intelligence and a flexibility in how we interact with one another, while keeping a steady course with respect to the others involved in the project. This has required mutual trust and conviction as to our own capabilities and the goodwill of others.

In addition to this, we have dared to talk about our different ways of functioning and, ultimately, make them a strength. For example, one of us has the tendency to say things in a more synthetic fashion, using few words – sometimes too few perhaps. The other has a tendency to express things in a more detailed fashion; so talking more. We have been able to capitalize on that difference: *in one particular situation, it is better that one of us takes the lead, and in another situation, the other of us goes first.* Or, during a conference for example, we mix both to reach more people.

Another source of synergy between us has been to engage in the process of "intervision" as soon as something comes up. One of us will say *something is happening to me. I need your help to talk and exchange: what do you think?* The fact of knowing that we will kindly tell each other whatever we have to and to give honest feedback has created a profound level of trust and authenticity.

Finally, we have learned to take into account the "I" and the "We" with confidence ... avoiding misplaced "ego" dynamics. We signed all of our messages and reports to PERICEO group members with our two first names as referents; both of us able to answer any questions from other members of the group with equal authority. At meetings with the whole group, one of us could be absent without worrying that the other would try to take over her place. At workshops or conferences, each of us takes account of the other's needs and values her input. No egocentricity.

And today? We desire to go further together, to use this tool, to train and to give presentations about what we have learned through this process.

Another factor that has allowed us to stay the course and to continue the project has been the support we received from Robert Dilts and Gilles Roy. Certainly, as we mentioned earlier in this book, we share with them the passion for Collective Intelligence and our commitment to explore and experiment with new socio-professional paradigms. Our interest in writing also links us. We relied on their support when we had to orchestrate our energy, face challenges, rebound in the face of certain difficulties and, in the end, have good level of perseverance," This brings up the importance of leadership in any collective work!

We scheduled regular appointments with Robert and Gilles, or made them spontaneously if necessary. Their supervision and their kindness has consistently supported and encouraged us.

For those who know him, Robert embodies a quality of being that makes you grow. His ability to "walk the talk" has given us inspiration to pursue what we want to embody, and even greater determination to persevere in following through with this project. To be recommended by him touches us deeply.

As for Gilles, in addition to his generosity, he embodies a sense of realism and critical thinking that has systematically enabled us to move forward: indicating exactly what needed to be reviewed, improved, etc. Once again, we have experienced that "the people who are here are the right ones!"

Thank you very much.

Elisabeth Falcone and isabelle Meiss - March 2018

Dilts Strategy Group and SFM™

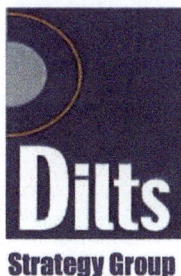

The *Dilts Strategy Group* is a consulting, coaching and training company with an international network of consultants in more than 25 countries. Co-founded by Robert Dilts and his brother John Dilts, the purpose of the Dilts Strategy Group (DSG) is to combine proven business criteria with strategic knowledge and behavioral skills, through the Success Factor Modeling Process (SFM™), in order to support the growth and development of individuals and organizations on many levels. DSG's services include: modeling, training, consulting, coaching and hosting seminars and conferences in the application of SFM ™.

* **Vision:** *A world in which people are fulfilling their aspirations and giving the best of themselves to produce a positive systemic impact through their ventures* – More and more organizations, businesses and projects that promote the growth and mastery of the those involved and create a more healthy, harmonious and thriving planet and society.

* **Mission:** *To discover and share the "differences that make a difference" in creating and growing successful ventures* – Identifying and transmitting the key success factors necessary to build a sustainable and successful business, team or project.

* **Ambition:** *To be a globally recognized pioneer and a leader in holistic business strategy* – A respected source of methods, models and tools that strongly and positively influence the way teams, businesses and organizations around the world are managed and led.

> * **Role:** *An international group of consultants and coaches with experience in NLP and enterprise who collaborate to provide effective business strategies and appropriate support* – A network of forward thinking and entrepreneurial people who work together to help teams, businesses and organizations and support each other to significantly improve their performances in the areas of entrepreneurship, leadership, innovation, collective intelligence and communication.

http://www.diltsstrategygroup.com

Success Factor Modeling (SFM™)

Success Factor Modeling™ (SFM) was developed by Robert and John Dilts as a method to identify and transfer the critical success factors necessary to promote the growth and impact of individuals, teams and organizations, and to help them be maximally prepared to create, recognize and take advantage of opportunities when they arise. By examining successful businesses, projects and initiatives and observing the behavior of high-performing individuals and teams, SFM™ helps people and organizations to quantify the factors that have created their legacy of success and to identify the trends necessary to extend that legacy into the future. These factors can then be "baked into" people's daily activities by identifying and extending what they are already doing that is successful.

Success Factor Modeling™ is founded upon a set of principles and distinctions which are uniquely suited to analyze and identify crucial patterns of *business practices* and *behavioral skills* used by successful individuals, teams and companies. The SFM™ process is used to identify the critical success factors employed by successful entrepreneurs, teams and business leaders and then to define specific models, tools and skills that can be used by others to greatly increase their chances of producing impact and achieving success.

Behavior modeling involves observing and mapping the crucial mental and physical processes which underlie an exceptional performance of some type. The goal of the behavior modeling process is to identify the essential elements of thought and action required by an individual or group to produce the desired response or outcome. It is the process of taking a complex performance or interaction and breaking it into small enough chunks so that it can be recapitulated in some way. The purpose of behavior modeling is to create a pragmatic map or "model" of that behavior which can be used to reproduce or simulate some aspect of that performance by anyone who is motivated to do so. Thus, it involves benchmarking behaviors and ideas, as well as business practices. (See *Modeling with NLP*, Dilts, R., 1998.)

Success Factor Modeling can be likened to identifying the particular key needed to unlock the door to success for various life situations. Life circumstances present us with doorways leading to different areas of success. The locks on these doorways are the critical issues and contextual constraints we must address in order to reach our goal in those particular circumstances. The "key" to a particular "lock" is the appropriate combination of behaviors and the corresponding mindset required to effectively address the issues and constraints presented by a certain context.

A key that successfully unlocks one door will not necessarily unlock another one, even if it worked perfectly for the previous door. Thus, in order to address changing contexts, an effective model would provide not only a description of the key, but also include a description of the lock which that key fits.

Thus, the objective of the SFM™ process is to make an instrumental map—one supported by a variety of exercises, formats and tools that allows people to apply the factors that have been modeled in order to reach key outcomes within their chosen context. To accomplish this, SFM applies the following basic template:

MINDSET
(How we think)

PRODUCES

ACTIONS
(What we do)

CREATES

OUTCOMES
(What we achieve)

The Basic Success Factor Modeling Template

Our *mindset*—which is made up of our inner state, attitude and thinking processes—produces outer behavioral actions. It is our mindset that determines what we do and the type of *actions* we take in a particular situation. These actions, in turn, create *outcomes* in the external world around us. Achieving desired outcomes in our environment thus requires the proper mindset in order to produce the necessary and appropriate actions.

Desired outcomes, then, are the "locks" an individual is seeking to successfully open. The individual's mindset and actions form the "key" which will open a particular lock. The goal of Success Factor Modeling is to find the proper "keys" which open the "locks" necessary to reach our desired outcomes.

Appendix 1

Presentation of the co-authors and the illustrator

Robert DILTS has had a global reputation as a leading coach, behavioral skills trainer and business consultant since the late 1970s.

A major developer and expert in the field of Neuro-Linguistic Programming (NLP), Robert has provided coaching, consulting and training throughout the world to a wide variety of individuals and organizations.

Together with his brother John, Robert pioneered the principles and techniques of Success Factor Modeling (SFM™); he has authored numerous books and articles about how they may be applied to enhance leadership, creativity, communication and team development.

Robert's recent book series on Success Factor Modeling identifies key characteristics and capabilities shared by successful entrepreneurs, teams and ventures. *Next Generation Entrepreneurs* (2015) presents models, tools, exercises, illustrations and case examples – of both world famous and everyday entrepreneurs – in order to help readers understand how to build a "Circle of Success" and create a business aligned with their life purpose. *Generative Collaboration* (2016) helps people to increase their capacity for working effectively together with others and to experience the excitement, satisfaction and power of collective intelligence. *Conscious Leadership and Resilience* (2017) supports people to become increasingly authentic, emotionally intelligent, purposeful and responsible, and to create teams and ventures that are more productive, ecological, sustainable and fun.

His book *Visionary Leadership Skills* draws from Robert extensive study of historical and corporate leaders; it presents the tools and skills necessary for "creating a world to which people want to belong ". *Alpha Leadership: Tools for Business Leaders Who Want More From Life* (with Ann Deering and Julian Russell) captures and shares the latest practices of effective leadership, offering approaches to reduce stress and to promote satisfaction. *From Coach to Awakener* provides a road map and set of toolboxes for coaches to help clients reach goals on a number of different levels of learning and change. *The Hero's Journey: A Voyage of Self Discovery* (with Stephen Gilligan) s about how to reconnect you with your deepest calling, transform limiting beliefs and habits and improve self-image.

Robert's recent book series on *Success Factor Modeling* identifies key characteristics and capabilities shared by successful entrepreneurs, teams and ventures. *Next Generation Entrepreneurs* (2015) presents models, tools, exercises, illustrations and case examples – of both world famous and everyday entrepreneurs – in order to help readers understand how to build a "Circle of Success" and create a business aligned with their life purpose. *Generative Collaboration* (2016) helps people to increase their capacity for working effectively together with others and to experience the excitement, satisfaction and power of collective intelligence. *Conscious Leadership and Resilience* (2017) supports people to become increasingly authentic, emotionally intelligent, purposeful and responsible, and to create teams and ventures that are more productive, ecological and sustainable.

Past corporate clients and sponsors have included Apple Computer, Microsoft, Hewlett-Packard, IBM, Lucasfilms Ltd. and the State Railway of Italy. He has lectured extensively on coaching, leadership, innovation, collective intelligence, organizational learning and change management, making presentations and keynote addresses for The International Coaching Federation (ICF), HEC Paris, The United Nations, The World Health Organization, Harvard University and the International University of Monaco. In 1997 and 1998, Robert supervised the design of Tools for Living, the behavior management portion of the program used by Weight Watcher's International.

Robert was an associate professor at the ISVOR Fiat School of Management for more than fifteen years, helping to develop programs on leadership, innovation, values and systemic thinking. From 2001–2004 he served as chief scientist and Chairman of the Board for ISVOR DILTS Leadership Systems, a joint venture with ISVOR Fiat (the former corporate university of the Fiat Group) that delivered a wide range of innovative leadership development programs to large corporations on a global scale.

A co-founder of Dilts Strategy Group, Robert was also founder and CEO of Behavioral Engineering, a company that developed computer software and hardware applications emphasizing behavioral change. Robert has a degree in Behavioral Technology from the University of California at Santa Cruz.

Elisabeth FALCONE is a trainer, consultant, coach and facilitator.

Her passion is creating bridges between individuals and groups.

Her mission is to help both groups and individuals to get to the best of themselves, boosting their performance and fulfilling their calling.

Elisabeth began her career as a management supervisor in national and international groups, enabling her to understand the overall functioning of big organizations and the various "levers and brakes" involved.

She has always been passionate about human and social sciences and neurosciences. She worked extensively in sectors with marked diversity - intercultural, gender, generational equity, disability, etc. Believing that the greatest strength and weakness of any organization is its human capital, Elisabeth has created a venture called *The HR Difference*, in response to an emerging need in our society: the fulfillment of each for the happiness and benefit of all.

The venture, based in the south of France, has set itself the mission of renovating the entrepreneurial spirit, in which profit becomes a means of contributing to the progress of a more humane, peaceful and respectful society committed to the common good.

How?

Assisting individuals and organizations with issues related to:

* Collective Intelligence.

* Diversity.

* Conscious Leadership.

* Personal development.

* Happiness at work.

Through training, coaching, facilitation and consulting.

Elisabeth is also a writer, lecturer and trainer, and has collaborated with different partners who share the same vision and commitment, including Dilts Strategy Group and Vision 2021, of which she was a co-founder.

She is a partner approved by the Dilts Strategy Group in France.

Her professional qualifications include:

* Coach – Associate Member, French Coaching Society.

* NLP Master Practitioner and Trainer – Society of NLP.

* Certified Facilitator of Collective Intelligence (SFM2) and Conscious Leadership (SFM3) by Robert Dilts – Member of the Dilts Strategy Group Leadership Team.

* Certified in Generative Consulting – I.A.G.C.

To contact her:

www.elisabethfalcone.com

www.ladifferencerh.com

+33(0)6.75.20.62.83

Isabelle MEISS is a consultant, coach and facilitator.

Her passion: The dance of human relations

Her mission: To contribute to the development and the expression of interpersonal skills to create successful collaborations that make sense to individuals and organizations.

For more than 25 years, Isabelle has contributed to streamlining the flow of information in B-to-B communication (including sectors such as: NICT, Audit and Consulting, HR, business law, and construction). In particular, through her work as a leadership communications manager (EMC – today Dell-EMC) and senior consultant, she has managed corporate communication projects relating to the different phases of corporate life-cycle and trained experts and managers in media relations.

Integrating her work experience with other professional trainings, Isabelle assists individuals and organizations to improve their capacity for well-being and collaboration. She has been coaching since 2006 and, since 2010, has been assisting individuals, teams and organizations in change management, by facilitating their communication and helping them to manage and develop better relationships and collaboration through:

* Individual and collective coaching of experts, managers, startups, teams, trainers and graduates.

* Facilitation of groups and teams to support change.

* Development of relational skills.

* Support in management of communication and press relations projects.

Isabelle also works as a professional translator and has translated into French, in collaboration with a colleague, Robert Dilts' book series *Success Factor Modeling* (SFM™): *Next Generation Entrepreneurs, Generative Collaboration,* and *Conscious Leadership and Resilience.*

Isabelle considers life itself to be a journey of learning, empowerment and evolution. Innovation and human relationships energize her as well as the pleasure of the renewed discovery of others during interactions. Convinced that individuals can enrich themselves through their differences and collaboration, she contributes to building bridges by promoting the expression of the best of each person in contexts that support evolution and transformation.

Isabelle works in collaboration with complementary partners and sponsors, including the Dilts Strategy Group; Ambroise conseil, a guidance and consulting agency specialized in developing innovation and people (www.ambroiseconseil.com); Mozaïk RH, the first French recruitment and human resources consultancy agency dedicated in promoting diversity (www.mozaïkrh.com); and Mute et Sens, a multidisciplinary ecosystem of experts serving the transition (www.muteetsens.org). She is also coach for the EASME - Executive Agency for SMEs – Set up by the European Commission (www.ec.europa.eu/easme/en); an active member of Vision 2021; and Com'unique l'authenticité, an association that has since 1996 been promoting approaches that facilitate knowledge and self-expression in the relationships, relying notably Non-violent Communication (www.com-unique.org).

Professional qualifications:

* Facilitating Collective Intelligence certification by Robert Dilts (2014), Career Change Check® coach accreditation by Promove TM (2012), young people coach certification by Elevatio (2010), NLP Master Practitioner certification by Society of NLP (2006), coach of business certification by FES (2006).

* Trainings in trainer profession (Demos,2011), skills assessment (Ambroise Conseil, 2012), systemic of organizations in change with Henry Roux de Bézieux (2007), communication and human relations consulting (AC and Associates multidisciplinary Cycle 1991-1995).

* Non-Violent communication (NVC) practitioner since 2003.

* Master in applied foreign languages for business and international affairs (English - Spanish) - Faculty of Letters and Human Sciences Besançon (1986).

Isabelle has danced since her childhood, practiced Qi Gong since 2002 and participated in Long hikes since 2010

To contact her:
www.ambroiseconseil.com
www.linkedin.com/in/isabelle-meiss-8599362
+33(0)6.17.50.50.64

Gilles Roy has been a trainer and HR consultant for thirty years in the south of France.

He became acquainted with Anglo-Saxon culture (two years in the USA, many stays in England) and specialized in the training and support of senior managers and management teams with an opening to systemic leadership and the principles of Collective Intelligence.

He was mayor of a small rural commune and helped to bring societal change to Haute Provence (in the form of organic farming, ecological renovation of communal buildings, reopening of the alternative education school system, development of handicrafts, systemic thinking, shared governance, etc.).

Gilles has been based in Avignon for 25 years, where he has created two companies with Marie-Paule Rous, "Formation Evolution et Synergie ", a training organization in NLP, Ericksonian Hypnosis, Coaching, Collective Intelligence, Brief Thérapies, etc. and "Rous and Roy Consulting" a network of consultants.

In partnership with Robert and Deborah Dilts, he developed the first training courses in Collective Intelligence in 2009. He is one of the founders of VISION 2021 and was its first President (from 2014-2017).

Influenced by his American colleagues, Gilles Roy began coaching in the late 1980s, while the concept did not yet exist in France.

He trained in coaching and NLP in the USA and England in the early 1990s, and became Master Trainer certified by INLPTA (Wyatt Woodsmall) and Society of NLP (Christina hall). He also trained in Neuro-Semantic and Méta-Coaching with ISNS (Michael Hall).

Since 1996, he has offered several training courses in Coaching every year in Provence and Switzerland and has trained several hundred people in this profession.

Also trained in personal psychology and psychotherapy, he served as psychotherapist and supervisor of psychotherapists. He holds a CEP (European Psychotherapist Certificate).

He is also holds a degree in Collective Intelligence, after having followed an university diploma course at the University of Cergy Pontoise.

In constant contact with the Anglo-Saxon world, Gilles Roy joined the ICF in 1997. He co-hosted an ICF satellite in Avignon between 2003 and 2005. He was also an associate member of the French Coaching Company from 1997 to 2017.

Gilles transitioned from supervising psychotherapists to supervising coaches in 2002.

He has himself been regularly supervised since 1998 and has experimented with different forms and styles of supervision.

He is currently supervised by Marianne CRAIG (MCC member ICF England).

He attended a coach training course in London with the CSA (Coaching Supervision Academy) Institute and obtained certification in June 2010. This training is accredited by ICF and EMCC. He is now part of CSA staff as guardian, trainer and Course Director. Since 2012, he has been training as coach supervisor CSA in France.

He was a member of AOCS (Association of Coaches Supervisors) based in England and is a member of the Professional Supervisors Federation (PSF) Board of Directors based in France.

Articles and publications

Gilles Roy wrote two books (self-published).

* Toi Puissance Trois (1995)

* Le Tao du Coaching (1998).

To contact him:

gilles.roy2@orange.fr.

Antonio Meza is an alchemist of the collective imagination. From an early age in Mexico, he has been fascinated by mythology, symbols and everything that creates links between the most diverse people.

A draftsman by birth, and a storyteller by passion, he is trained in the plastic arts and the cinema, but also in the techniques of organizational communication.

In Paris, he studied coaching and training and has been a consultant, trainer, facilitator and coach since 2008. He has conducted more than 250 workshops in inter-cultural communication, decision-making, emotional intelligence, generative collaboration, storytelling techniques and graphic facilitation.

As a speaker, in 2015 he won first prize at Toastmasters International's international public speaking contest at the European level and was invited to deliver his speech "Le Miroir" at the TEDx Clermont-Ferrand conference.

Antonio also uses his skills as an illustrator artist to offer graphic facilitation at brainstorming seminars, conferences and sessions for companies such as Sanofi, Thales, Adidas and Louis Vuitton.

As a cartoonist, Antonio illustrated 6 books including "*Next Generation Entrepreneurs*" (Robert Dilts 2015) and "*Les vrais secrets de la communication*" (Béatrice Arnaud, 2015); he has also produced animated videos to explain complex ideas with a simple and humorous language.

Antonio speaks fluently and works in French, English and Spanish. He can converse in Italian and order a beer in German. He lives in Issy les Moulineaux in Paris with his wife Susanne and his cats Ronia and Atreju.

To contact him:
www.antoons.net
hola@antoons.net
Instagram and twitter: @antonsparis

Presentation of Training Evolution and Synergy (FES)

FES has been a professional training organization serving individuals and organizations since 1990. Its main working methods are NLP, coaching, Collective Intelligence, Ericksonian Hypnosis and Brief Therapy.

ACTION

We help our clients, through consultations, training and on-site support, to meet the following challenges:

* To acquire excellent communication skills,

* To be able to manage the challenges of change and identity crisis,

* To define and achieve their objectives,

* To evaluate and optimize their potential,

* To succeed in whatever they undertake,

* To recognize and implement their "mission in life".

VISION

Our vision is to build bridges between the present and the future allowing human beings to find meaning, to give meaning and to awaken their essence.

This humanist perspective assumes that personal development and professional efficiency are complementary and mutually reinforcing: we are the creators of our lives.

MISSION

* Offering effective communication tools,

* Providing education for innovative change,

* Helping to establish win-win relationships,

* Enabling more humane companies and societies to emerge,

  * Succeeding in helping others.

STRENGTHS

1. Education and practice are constantly being updated

Although we are already regarded as one of the best specialists in our industry, we continue to train and participate in research teams. We are constantly testing new approaches to provide the highest level of quality and service.

2. Real availability

Our administrative capabilities and our personal organization allow us to be easily contactable and available.

We personally monitor the progress of our trainees and clients, not only during training or interventions, but also between sessions and even beyond for those who so wish.

3. Tailor-made training and interventions

Depending on your needs, whether you are an isolated person, a team or a company of several hundred people, we can offer you tailor-made training or interventions, whose content, form, cost and duration we define together.

4. International synergy and certifications

We maintain a network within all French-speaking countries (Belgium, Switzerland, Maghreb, etc.) and also in England and the USA. We regularly invite the most well-known trainers, consultants, psychotherapists etc., in relation to the disciplines we teach.

The certifications in NLP, Coaching and Hypnosis that we issue are validated by Society of NLP and the NLPNL association.

e-mail: formationevolutionetsynergie@wanadoo.fr
website: www.coaching-pnl.com

VISION 2021 presentation: Collective Intelligence in Action

The mission of Vision 2021 is to explore and disseminate collaborative practices in Collective Intelligence for the harmonious development of human societies.

Composed of about 100 members, including coaches and consultants but also managers, civil servants, entrepreneurs, etc., Vision 2021 promotes Collective Intelligence as one of the ways to improve the performance of teams, groups, businesses and organizations.

The association brings together pragmatic people of good will, driven by a positive vision of the future.

Most active members of the association have professional activities involving the dissemination of Collective Intelligence in different forms (advisory services, teams, training and conferences, books, games, etc.). They are responsible for many initiatives that complement the activities of the association.

Concrete achievements

* An annual congress. That of 2016 was attended by 330 participants and that of 2017 nearly 500. In 2019 there were 680 participants.

* The Summer University (at the end of August).

* Articles in the two White Papers on Collective Intelligence published by *Colligence* (2014 and 2015).

* A Newsletter (for our people).

* Monitoring and coordination of working groups and research groups, such as PERICEO – the one responsible for this book.

Projects

* A major World Congress in France in 2021.

* Publication of a specific White Paper *Vision 2021*.

* Experience-sharing seminars.

> * Establishment of a research center in Provence.

> * Identification of sponsors and partners to finance and support projects relating to collective intelligence.

> * The development of satellite groups in France (Lyon, Paris, Réunion etc.). and internationally.

Current Work Groups

> * PERICEO: Group modeling of success factors that support the development of Collective Intelligence in organizations; based on interviews with managers and leaders.

> * ICI 3D: A research group for the development of a software to analyze the operation of collective intelligence in organizations.

> * IC and Consciousness: Research groups on the theme of the link between spirituality and collective intelligence.

> * IC LAB: A local research and experimentation group for Collective Intelligence. The first is based in Avignon, and the plan is to spread out to wherever there is interest.

> * Growing and Progressing in IC: A work Group on Collective Intelligence Education.

Other initiatives

Vision 2021 also promotes events and projects that are aligned with its mission, such as:

> * The 5Rythms dance practice to set Collective Intelligence in motion, with Deborah Bacon Dilts.

> * U for Youth, work, applying Otto Scharmer's teachings for children, adolescents and parents, with Mia Boutemy.

* **The VISION**: The emergence of a more harmonious world to which everyone wants to belong.

* **The MISSION**: To experiment and spread the power of generative collaboration and put Collective Intelligence into action.

* **The AMBITION**: To become ambassadors and key players in Collective Intelligence.

* **The ROLE**: To be an inspiring team of transformers for the deployment of Collective Intelligence worldwide.

We are trying to best express what we are advocating by working in a very collegial way, relying on a board of directors that meets monthly and practices 'delegated meetings', where facilitation and functions are taken in turn by each member of the board of directors.

Each year, specific project teams are formed to organize major events such as the Collective Intelligence Congress and the Summer University. They operate independently and inform the Vision 2021 Management Board of their progress.

HOW TO GET MORE INFORMATION OR JOIN THE ASSOCIATION?

Email: contact@vision-2021.com

Website: www.vision-2021.com.

Appendix 4

Overview of the PERICEO project

Study "How effective teams and organizations promote and utilize Collective Intelligence".

What is the subject of the study?

Global economic changes have forced teams and organizations to change their way of operating so that they can do more with less resources. The purpose of this study has been to make a field-based evaluation of the latest trends and ideas applied by high performing teams and organizations to promote synergies and develop Collective Intelligence in order to address the challenges and take advantage of opportunities in the current economic environment. The information gathered during this study will help to determine how to increase productivity, profitability and satisfaction. The main trends emerging will be reflected in articles to be published in a selected journals specializing in business and innovation.

What is the Dilts Strategy Group (DSG)?

The *Dilts Strategy Group* is a network of specially trained consultants providing coaching, training and other development services to companies throughout the world. It offers both strategic consulting and coaching to its clients, customers and partners. Through its strategic consulting activity, DSG helps customers grow and take advantage of new opportunities by identifying their strengths and areas for improvement. DSG provides training programs, coaching and consulting for companies ranging from new start-ups to multinational organizations.

Robert Dilts, founder of Dilts Strategy Group and supervisor of this study, has extensive experience in modeling excellence. He has developed the principles and techniques of "Success Factor Modeling", which is the topic of his forthcoming book, and authored over 20 other books about how these principles and techniques may be applied to enhance leadership, creativity, communication and team development. His books include *Visionary Leadership Skills, Alpha Leadership, From Coach to Awakener, Skills for the Future* and *Strategies of Genius*. Dilts has been studying and teaching principles and methods of leadership, entrepreneurship, collective intelligence and generative collaboration for the past decade drawing upon his studies of such companies as Apple, IBM, Google, Lucasfilms and Disney.

What do we mean by Collective Intelligence?

Working together with others in groups and teams is an increasingly important part of modern business success. High functioning groups and teams demonstrate the characteristic of collective intelligence; a phenomenon that greatly enhances both efficiency and creativity. Intelligence is defined as: The ability to interact successfully with one's world, especially in the face of challenge or change. Collective intelligence has to do with a shared or group intelligence that emerges from the collaboration and communication between individuals in groups and other interacting systems.

Practically speaking, collective intelligence relates to the ability of individuals in a team or group to share knowledge and think and act in an aligned and coordinated fashion to achieve critical outcomes. In organizations, this involves the process of people working cooperatively to reach common objectives by exchanging information and complementing one another's skills and experience. This accumulation and integration of individual know-how and competence also serves as a platform from which to develop new insights, ideas and capabilities. As a result, a major benefit of promoting collective intelligence is that group members grow more quickly and the creative problem solving capacity of the organization is improved through increased access to knowledge and expertise.

Participants of the study

Dilts Strategy Group will contact a number of teams and companies to participate in interviews and other activities ranging from one hour to several days. These teams and companies will be selected on the basis of their reputation as a strong leader among peers

Topics addressed:

* What are the current challenges and opportunities the company or team is facing?

* How do companies or teams define collective intelligence?

* How do they view and value Collective Intelligence as a key means to succeed in today's business environment?

* How do they modify their business strategies and their management practices to encourage and develop Collective Intelligence?

* What specific steps have they implemented to support Collective Intelligence on a practical level?

Advantages for participating teams and companies:

* The participants will receive direct, confidential and personal feedback on their strengths in Collective Intelligence as they will appeared in relation to the other teams and organizations studied.

* They will receive direct feedback on the significant ideas and trends that have been developed by other teams and organizations in similar situations.

* They will have the opportunity to interact with experienced consultants in the areas of leadership, innovation and development.

* They will receive the results of the investigation before publication.

Ethics

The consultants of the Dilts Strategy Group network undertake to respect the following rules:

* Place the individuals and teams of the companies involved in the study at the center of the study.

* Work on the basis of the shared questionnaire defined by the members of the PERICEO project;

* Respect the free choice of the participants in the investigation;

* Ensure the confidentiality of the information collected during the investigation;

   * Ensure proper transmission of data to the PERICEO project team;

   * Commit to participating in scheduled meetings;

   * Get involved in the actions implemented by the PERICEO project team

   * Commit to the principles of the Charter and Ethical Code for the Collective Intelligence Study. (See pages 84-85,)

Confidentiality rules

More specifically, the information collected in the study will be treated confidentially according to the following rules:

   * The content of the interviews will be strictly confidential and will be shared exclusively within the Dilts Strategy Group study group for analysis purposes only.

   * Each participant will receive direct, confidential and personal feedback on the strengths that have been identified in relation to the other teams and organizations. This feedback will remain private and confidential.

   * Information published in the form of publications or press articles will be summaries of trends in a significant number of interviews. No mention of conclusions specific to a company or department of that company will be published unless a specific agreement has been concluded with both the company and the department in question.

   * In this case, the company or department remains master of the text, in the sense that nothing will be published before obtaining its formal agreement on the text. The company or department therefore freely exercises a full right of scrutiny over the content of the testimony.

Appendix 5

Charter and Ethical Code for the Collective Intelligence PERICEO Study

For the consultants involved in PERICEO

Title 1: Consultants' duties

Art.1.1: Intervention

Consultants will apply what they have learned through their training, experience, supervision or intervision, and sharing of practices.

Art.1.2: Confidentiality

Consultants are bound by professional discretion.

Art.1.3: Supervision

Consultants are to seek supervision whenever the situation requires it.

Art.1.4: Respect for people

Conscious of their position, consultants will refrain from any abuse of their influence.

Art.1.5: Obligation of means

Consultants shall use all means needed to carry out their assignment, including, if necessary, involving other colleagues.

Title 2: The duties of consultants towards interviewees

Article 2.1: Place of the interviewees

Consultants must pay attention to the meaning and effects of the situation and reputation of interviewees.

Article 2.2: Responsibility

Consultants leave all responsibility for actions and decisions to the interviewees.

Article 2.3: Request made

The consultants shall ensure that their approach is consistent with the expectations or challenges expressed by the interviewees and their organization.

Article 2.4: Personal protection

Consultants adapt their approach with respect to the needs of the interviewees.

Title 3: The duties of consultants towards the organization

Article 3.1: Protecting organizations

The consultants are attentive to the profession, uses, culture, context and constraints of the organization that invites them.

Article 3.2: Reporting

The consultants shall report on the progress of their assignment only to their PERICEO project supervisor.

Title 4: The duties of consultants towards their colleagues

Article 4.1: Obligation of discretion

Consultants are to maintain appropriate discretion with respect to their colleagues.

Questions for PERICEO interviews

1) Vision

Vision refers to people's view of the larger system of which they are part. It provides the overall direction of the team and defines the purpose of its interactions (*for whom or for what* a specific action or direction has been undertaken?).

* What is the organization's vision? How has it been communicated?

* To what extent does this vision determine the implementation of Collective Intelligence?

* How does the implementation of Collective Intelligence support the vision?

2) The sense of Identity

Identity is related to people's sense of their role and mission. These factors relate to *who* we are or perceive ourselves to be.

* How would you describe the identity and mission of the team – before implementing Collective Intelligence and after?

* How has Collective Intelligence been used to define "who you are collectively"?

* What image, symbol or metaphor would best match the identity of the team and its mission?

3) Values and Beliefs

Values and beliefs provide the reinforcement that supports or inhibits particular capabilities and actions. They relate to *why* a particular path is taken and the deeper motivations which drive people to act or persevere. Values, and related beliefs, determine how events and communications are interpreted and given meaning. Thus, they are the key to motivation and culture.

* What are the key values that been established to foster Collective Intelligence (provide a list of values if necessary)?

* What are the beliefs that support and motivate team members when it comes to developing and applying Collective Intelligence?

4) Core skills and capabilities

Capabilities refer to mental maps, plans and strategies that support the implementation of collective intelligence. They direct *how* actions are chosen and carried out.

* What specific skills and capabilities (leadership, communication, conflict resolution etc.) are most important in order to implement Collective Intelligence?

* How are these skills transmitted / taught?

* What strategies have been defined in order to foster and implement greater Collective Intelligence?

5) Specific actions and behaviors

Behavioral factors are the specific actions undertaken to achieve success. They involve *what* specifically must be done or accomplished in order to succeed.

* What were and are the most important actions taken to promote Collective Intelligence?

* What behaviors have been and are most essential in order to nurture and implement Collective Intelligence?

6) Environmental opportunities and influences

Environmental factors determine external opportunities or constraints for Collective Intelligence; i.e., *where and when* Collective Intelligence occurs.

* What were and are the environment-related factors most significant in order to foster and sustain Collective Intelligence?

* Which environmental factors create constraints to the development of Collective Intelligence?

* What are the most significant environmental factors that provide the greatest opportunities to develop Collective Intelligence?

Robert DILTS, November 2013, revised and increased by the PERICEO Group, February 2014.

Appendix 7

The PERICEO training program

PERICEO: The Tool

Teams and organizations, two days to learn to diagnose and develop your Collective Intelligence capabilities

The objectives of the training

* To present a tool for diagnosing the current level of Collective Intelligence in an organization.

* To optimize individual and collective awareness and functioning with respect to Collective Intelligence.

* To understand and to master the PERICEO tool.

* To understand the underlying models and "philosophy" behind the tool: logical levels - modeling - key factors - scorecards.

* To raise awareness of the various types of listening, questioning, language patterns, perceptual positions and principles that promote Collective Intelligence: e.g., 'The Map is not territory '...

Pedagogical method

* A pragmatic and constructive approach.

* The trainer's conceptual inputs.

* Realization of a case study: the participants are invited to implement what they learned in training within a company, community, association or group of their choice.

* Modeling workshops.

* Supervision.

* Participants' self-assessment.

* Pedagogical support - Glossary - Presentation of the framework of the tool.

Public addressed

> * Executives, managers and employees wishing to promote the development of Collective Intelligence within their team or organization and have a simple and efficient diagnostic tool.

Terms

> * Two days during which we will help you to diagnose your organization according to the input gathered from the training or supervision sessions.

Price

> * Contact us or send an e-mail:
> info@periceo.com

Day one - Learning the underlying models

> * Getting acquainted with the philosophy of NLP and the underlying models:
>
>   - A few basic principles.
>
>   - Dilts pyramid: presentation, operation and alignment of logical levels.
>
>   - Clarification of the concepts of purpose - identity - values and beliefs - capabilities - behaviors - environment.
>
>   - Modeling - The key factors.
>
>   - The Scorecards.
>
> * Vision - Mission - Ambition - Role: for an individual, a group,an organization.

Day 2 - Understanding and using the tool

* Understand the process that led to the development of the tool: ongoing research and development.

* Presentation of key factors by level.

* The importance of language.

* Implementation with respect to a specific case: conduct the interview - complete the score cards - feedback - meaning and analysis.

Action planning and personal resources

* And now?

* Implementation of a personal action plan by each trainee following his or her learning and awareness.

* The possible follow-up options for the organization.

To contact us,

e-mail: info@periceo.com

Telephone:

* Elisabeth Falcone + 33 (0)6 75 20 62 83
* Isabelle Meiss + 33 (0)6 17 50 50 64

Bibliography

* Aurégan, P., Joffre, P., Loilier, T., & Tellier, A., *Exploration prospective et management stratégique: vers une approche projet de la stratégie.* Management & Future, 2008.

* Bateson, G., *Vers une écologie de l'esprit. Tome 1.* Paris : Seuil, 1976.

* Beck & Cowan *Spiral Dynamics: mastering values leadership and change.* US: Wiley and Blackwell publisher, 1995.

* Berry t. & Swimme b ., *The universe story.* San Francisco: Harper, 1992.

* Brown, j ., *The world café: shaping our future through conversations that matter.* San Francisco: Berrett-Koehler publishers, 2005.

* Chapelle G., Gérard T.E, Simon M., Marsan C., Lavens J., Saint-Girons S., Julien Eric, *L'Intelligence Collective : co-créons en conscience le monde de demain.* Yves Michel Editions, 2014

* Damon j ., *Gaston Berger (1896-1960).* Informations Sociales, 2005.

* Dilts R. (illustrated by Antonio Meza), *Success Factor Modeling Volume II: Generative Collaboration - Releasing the Creative Power of Collective Intelligence.* Dilts Strategy Group, Santa Cruz CA, 2016.

* Dilts R. (illustrations Antonio Meza), *La Modélisation des Facteurs de Succès Tome II: Collaboration Générative – Libérer la puissance créative de L'Intelligence Collective.* Dilts Strategy Group, Santa Cruz, CA, 2018.

* Dilts R. (illustrated by Antonio Meza), *Success Factor Modeling Volume I: Next Generation Entrepreneurs - Live Your Dreams and Make a Better World through Your Business.* Dilts Strategy Group, Santa Cruz, CA, 2015.

* Dilts R. (Antonio Meza), *Success Factor Modeling Volume I: Entrepreneurs Nouvelle Génération – Vivez Vos*

Rêves et Créez un Monde Meilleur par Votre Entreprise. Dilts Strategy Group, Santa Cruz, CA, 2017.

* Dilts R. (illustrated by Antonio Meza). *Success Factor Modeling, Volume III - Conscious Leadership and Resilience: Orchestrating innovation and Fitness for the Future.* Dilts Strategy Group, Santa Cruz, CA, 2017. Translation into French to appear.

* Dilts R ., *Modeling with NLP.* Meta Publications, Capitola, CA, 1998.

* Dilts R., *Modéliser avec la PNL.* Dunod-InterEditions, Paris, France, 2004

* Dilts R., *Skills for the Future.* Meta publications, Capitola, CA, 1993.

* Dilts R.,*Des outils pour l'avenir,* La Méridienne, Paris, France, 1995.

* Dilts R ., *From Coach to Awakener.* Dilts Strategy Group, Santa Cruz, CA, 2018, 2003.

* Dilts R., *Être coach : de la recherche de la performance à l'éveil.* Dunod-InterEditions, Paris, France, 2008.

* Dilts R. and DeLozier J., *Encyclopedia of Systemic Neuro-Linguistic Programming and NLP New Coding.* NLP University Press, Santa Cruz, CA, 2000.

* Gaudin T., *Responsabilité et Environnement.* Risque et prospective, 2010

* Gaudin T., *La prospective.* Paris : University Press of France, 2013.

* Gauthier A., *Le co-leadership évolutionnaire.* Auxerre: H Diffusion (collection Précussions), 2013.

* Godet M., *Manuel de prospective stratégique, Tome 1.* Paris : Dunod, 2009

* Graves W., *The never ending quest.* US: Eclett Publishing, 2005.

* Hilts S. & Turoff M., *The Network Nation.* US, 1993.

* Isaacs w ., *Dialogue: the art of thinking together.* New York: Crown business publishers, 2009.

* Kahane a ., *Transformative scenario planning: working together to change the future* (1st ed.). San Francisco: Berrett-Koehler Publishers, 2012.

* Kahane A., *Pouvoir et amour.* Paris : Colligence Editions, 2015.

* Laloux R ., *Reinventing organizations.* Paris : Dateino, 2015.

* Le Bon G., *La psychologie des foules.* Paris, 1895.

* Lévy, P., *Intelligence collective.* Paris : La découverte, 2013.

* Malone, W. & Bernstein, M., *Handbook of Collective Intelligence.* US: MIT Press, 2015.

* Mousli, M. *Prospective et action publique.* L'Économie politique, 2013.

* North Whitehead A. (1929-1979). *Process and Reality.* US: Free Press

* Owen, H., *Open space technology : a user's guide.* San Francisco: Berrett-Koehler publishers, 2008.

* Payette a. & champagne C ., *Professional Co-Development Group.* Presse de l'Université du Québec (2005).

* Salais R., *La donnée n'est pas un donné: Pour une analyse critique de l'évaluation chiffrée de la performance.* Revue française d'administration publique, 2010.

* Scharmer O, *Theory U: leading from the future as it emerges : the social theory of presencing.* San Francisco: Berrett-Koehler Publishers, 2009.

* Scharmer O., *Leading from the emerging future.* San Francisco: Berret-Koehler publishers, 2013.

* Sheldrake R., *Reénchanter la Science.* Paris : Albin Michel, 2013.

* Sheldrake r ., *Seven Experiments That Could Change the World: a do-it-yourself guide to revolutionary science.* New York: Riverhead Books, 1995.

* Senge, p. (2006). *The fifth discipline.* London: Random House business publishers.

* Senge P., *Presence: Human purpose and the field of the future.* New York: Broadway business, 2008.

* Scouarnec A., *Plaidoyer pour un « renouveau » de la prospective.* Management & Future, 2008.

* Smith J. *Collective Intelligence in computer science.* US, 1994.

* Surowiecki J., *The Wisdom of Crowds.* Anchor Books, New York, NY, 2005.

* Surowiecki J., *La Sagesse Des Foules.* Jean-Claude Lattès, Paris France, 2008.

* Teilhard de Chardin P., *L'avenir de l'homme,* Oeuvres. Paris : Seuil, 1959.

* Weatley M. & Kellner-Rogers M., *A simpler way.* San Francisco: Berrett-Koehler publishers, 1996.

* Wilber K., *Une brève histoire de tout.* Montreal: Editions de Mortagne, 1997.

* Zobrist J. F., *Un petit patron naïf et paresseux.* Thionville: Stratégies et avenir, 2012.

www.ingramcontent.com/pod-product-compliance
Lightning Source LLC
Chambersburg PA
CBHW051259020426
42333CB00026B/3277